Discover Grammar

David Crystal

with classroom consultant

Geoff Barton

LONGMAN

Contents

1   Words   9

2   Sentences   21

3 Nouns and noun phrases   **67**

4 Verbs and verb phrases   **101**

5 Other kinds of word   **125**

6 Longer sentences and punctuation   **151**

How to use this book

Discover Grammar has been written to encourage you to experiment with the way language works, and to find out for yourself the way English uses different grammatical structures. It won't tell you everything there is to know about grammar. That would be impossible in a book of this size. But it does give you an introduction to the most important topics in the field.

The book divides the field of English grammar into 45 topics, and groups them into six parts. Most of the topics are handled in just two pages; a few take four or six pages. However, you'll find that the layout of the pages is always the same.

★ The left-hand page should be read first.

This provides the basic information about the topic. The right-hand page is headed Activities. It enables you to put into practice what you have learned on the left-hand page. You'll find that the Activities headed A are the easiest ones; and that they increase in difficulty as you move down the page.

★ The Activities are not an 'optional extra'.

They are an essential part of getting to grips with a topic. You can't understand grammar just by thinking about it: you have to carry out analyses, experiments, and surveys, just as you would in any other technical subject. You are not in control of a topic until you have done some work on the right-hand page.

★ The Activities have four chief roles:

- some help you check that you have understood the topic

- some suggest ways in which the topic relates to other fields of study, such as literature and science

- some suggest ways in which the topic can help you to develop your language skills generally

- and some are there to prove that grammar study can be fun.

Introduction

If you are a fluent speaker of English, in one of its many dialects, you already know everything that is in this book.

This shouldn't surprise you. If you've lived all your life in an English-speaking country, you began seriously listening to the language as soon as you were born, and you began to speak it at around age 1. Your grammar quickly grew. It took a few years to work out what all the rules were, and you made many errors along the way, but certainly, by the time you were 5, you had learned most of the rules of grammar that are described in this book – and more besides.

Learning the rules of grammar means being able to build sentences which have all the words in the right order, with the right endings, so that everything makes sense. It also means being able to recognize when the rules are being followed and when they are being broken. When a sentence is formed according to the rules of the language, we say it is **grammatical**. When a sentence breaks the rules, we say it is **ungrammatical**. This book tells you what the chief rules of grammar are.

The distinction between grammatical and ungrammatical sounds straightforward, but there are three complications.

★ If you have been brought up speaking a regional dialect of English, you might not know all the rules of grammar which are used in Standard English. Standard English is the variety of the language which is most widely used and understood throughout the English-speaking world. Your regional dialect may have rules of grammar which are different from those found in Standard English; and if this is so, you will need to learn the Standard English forms, especially when you write, if you want to be part of this wider community. This book is chiefly about the grammar of Standard English.

★ The rules of Standard English grammar vary a little, when people adapt their language to different situations. In particular, the rules which govern the way we speak are not exactly the same as those which govern the way we write. This book draws attention to these differences – and also to some of the distinctive ways in which Standard English is used in special situations, such as science and literature.

★ **Standard English** is for ever slowly changing. The language has changed dramatically since Anglo-Saxon times, and when we look at the works of Chaucer or Shakespeare we can see many differences in the rules of grammar. Changes are still taking place, at different rates, in different parts of the world. People therefore use grammar in slightly different ways, and do not all have the same views about what is the 'best' form of English to use. When people disagree about what is correct Standard English, we say there is a dispute over **usage**. This book draws attention to some of the chief disagreements about usage in the field of grammar.

Knowing about grammar

Even if you have been brought up speaking Standard English, you may not know how to talk about what you have learned. You will 'know grammar', but you may not 'know about' grammar. 'Knowing about' grammar means being able to talk about what it is you know. It is the same as 'knowing about' any other subject. When you learn biology, you learn a way of looking at living things; you learn how to describe them precisely; you learn the technical terms that belong to biology. It is the same with grammar. This book gives you a way of looking at English grammar, and introduces you to the chief technical terms that you need in order to describe the language precisely.

Why is it important to know about grammar? There are five chief reasons.

1 **Grammar is the foundation of a language.** It is not the largest part of a language (that distinction belongs to the vocabulary), nor is it the most noticeable part (that distinction belongs to spelling and pronunciation); but it **is** the most fundamental part. The grammar is the skeleton which makes everything hang together. Without grammar, we are left with a jumble of words and word–parts, and nothing makes sense.

2 **We are continually being urged to think carefully and critically about the way language is used around us.** Advertisers, politicians, lawyers, journalists, TV broadcasters, and many others are in the business of trying to give us an account of the world, to persuade us, or to sell us things, using language as their tool. They are experts in manipulating grammar to suit their purposes, and we must be experts too, if we want to see what those purposes are.

3 **The English language, as any language, is an object of great power, flexibility, and beauty.** It is a medium which provides us with vast areas of use to explore, especially in literature, and within which we ourselves can be endlessly creative. The more we know about how this medium works, to achieve its remarkable effects, the more we shall be able to appreciate it when people are using it well, and the more chance we shall have of improving our own use of it.

4 **Our language can let us down.** We can be tired, careless, or unthinking, and produce speech or writing which is ambiguous, imprecise, or downright unintelligible. To deal with these problems, we need to put language under the microscope, and work out what went wrong. Often, the diagnosis is a poor control of the rules of grammar.

5 **Learning about the grammar of English can help when you are learning other languages.** The more you know about the way words and sentences work in English, the more you will be able to see the relationships between English and other languages. You may, indeed, already know some terminology about grammar from learning a foreign language. That is a great start – but look out for differences.

The field of grammar

The field of grammar is divided into two main areas, one dealing with the analysis of **words**, the other with the analysis of **sentences**. The study of the form and structure of words is called **morphology**. The study of the form and structure of sentences is called **syntax**.

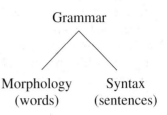

Grammar

Morphology   Syntax
(words)   (sentences)

★ Morphology

This term comes from ancient Greek: *morphe* meant 'form', so *morpho-logy* is basically 'the study of the form of something'. You will find the same term used in some other subjects. In biology, *morphology* refers to the form and structure of animals and plants. In earth science, *geomorphology* refers to the form and structure of the rocks making up the surface of the planet. In language study, *morphology* refers to the way words are formed and structured. Grammarians talk about a word's **morphological structure**, and the rules which tell us which word patterns are possible and which are not they call **morphological rules**. The chief patterns are described in Part 1.

★ Syntax

This term also came from ancient Greek, where *syn* meant 'together' and *tassein* meant 'arrange'. In grammar, the things which are 'arranged together' are words. We string words together so that we can express more complex ideas, producing the patterns we call phrases, clauses, and – most important of all – sentences. Grammarians talk about a sentence's **syntactic structure**, and the rules which tell us which sentence patterns are possible and which are not they call **syntactic rules**.

You may already have come across the term *syntax* in computer programming: if you have typed a string of words or symbols telling your computer to do something, and a message comes up on your screen, 'syntax error', it means there is a mistake somewhere in the structure of your command. The computer cannot recognize what you are trying to tell it. You will also find the term *syntax* used as a figure of speech in other subjects: a book called 'The Syntax of Cooking' is likely to be about the rules you need to know in order to be a good cook.

We begin to describe the syntactic structures of English in Part 2. In fact, most of this book is about the rules which underlie the patterns of syntax. Unlike such languages as French, German, and Latin, English makes very little use of morphology to show how words work together in sentences. There are only a few word-endings which are used in this way. But there is a great deal to say about English grammar under the heading of syntax.

Words

1 Words

There are hundreds of thousands of words in English, ranging from tiny items such as *a* to complex units such as *antidecentralization*. Each word has:

- a pronunciation
- a history
- a spelling
- a set of meanings

If you do not know how a word is pronounced or spelled, where it comes from, or what it means, you can find out by looking in the pages of a good **dictionary**. But what will you find out about words if you look in a **grammar**?

A grammar book tells you about the **structure** of words, or **word-formation**. In particular, it describes those features of word-formation which affect the way words work together to produce meaningful and acceptable sentences.

1 The parts of a word

Many words cannot be broken down into grammatical parts:

    yes   the   grammar   parrot   elephant

Some of these words have more than one syllable (*par-rot*, *e-le-phant*), but the syllables do not have a separate meaning. It does not make sense to ask 'What does the *phant* of *elephant* mean?' When a word has no meaningful parts, we say it consists only of a **base form**.

More complex words can be built up by adding other elements to the base form, each one having a separate meaning or use. These other elements are called **prefixes** and **suffixes**.

Prefixes

When we add a meaningful element **before** the base form, we call it a **prefix**. There are over 50 common prefixes in English.

- Some express the meaning 'not':

    wise → **un**wise   smoker → **non**-smoker   complete → **in**complete
    obey → **dis**obey   theist → **a**theist   modest → **im**modest

- Some express a notion of size or degree:

Increasing	Decreasing
sound → **mega**sound	normal → **sub**normal
market → **super**market	dog → **under**dog

- Several other meanings can be expressed by prefixes, such as:

    reversing an action: **dis**connect **de**frost **un**pack
    going wrong: **mal**function **pseudo**-scientific **mis**fire
    point of view: **anti**-perspirant **pro**-American **counter**-espionage
    time: **ex**-husband **fore**tell **pre**-war **ante**natal
    number: **bi**cycle **tri**cycle **mono**rail **uni**sex
    location: **inter**national **sub**way **fore**arm **trans**atlantic

Note that, with some prefixes, usage varies over whether to introduce a hyphen. For example, you will find both *anti-clockwise* and *anticlockwise* in dictionaries, and *tele-sales* as well as *telesales*.

Prefixes in English do not play an important role in making grammatical sentences. They are far more important in helping to build up your vocabulary.

Activities

A Add a prefix

Here is a list of base forms and a list of prefixes. Work out which forms go with which, then write a sentence to show how the words could be used. Note that some base forms allow the use of different prefixes.

skirt charge bishop flow belief fair
frost pilot grow work zero purpose

un- sub- co- over- mini- contra-
under- de- arch- multi- out- dis-

B Teach prefixes

Imagine you are a teacher of English as a foreign language, and you have to prepare a lesson on prefixes. Write a brief description of the meaning of each of the following prefixes, then show how the prefix is used by attaching it to three base forms, and use one of these new words in a sentence. The first one is done for you.

pre- When you add pre- to a base form, it means 'before' or 'in advance' of something.
preview, preschool, preheat
I'm going to write a preview of the school play.

1 post-   5 inter-   9 auto-
2 non-   6 pseudo-   10 semi-
3 hyper-   7 multi-
4 super-   8 vice-

C Analyse prefix sequences

The words in this list all use two prefixes.

● Try to identify the base form, and give it a definition (use a dictionary if you need to). Ignore any suffixes that may be present.

● Take each prefix and define its meaning.

● Now work out the meaning of the word as a whole by combining the meaning of each prefix with that of the base form.

● Compare your meaning with the meaning of the whole word given by a dictionary. How close did you get?

1 nonreusable   6 undiscouraged   11 reinflame
2 indecipherable   7 nonrecoverable   12 decompress
3 retransform   8 demisemiquaver   13 biodegradable
4 antiunemployment 9 rediscover   14 self-renewal
5 unsurpassed   10 nonremovable   15 autobiography

Suffixes

When we add a meaningful element **after** the base form of a word, we call it a **suffix**. Suffixes play an important role in constructing grammatical sentences in English – and most of them help to build up our vocabulary as well.

There are over 50 common suffixes in English. Most of them change one type of word into another. Look out for any changes in spelling, when the suffix is added.

- Some change verbs into nouns:

  break + -age → break**age**   amaze + -ment → amaze**ment**
  act + -or → act**or**

- Some make the meaning of a noun more abstract:

  spoon + -ful → spoon**ful**   race + -ism → rac**ism**
  friend + -ship → friend**ship**

Several other functions can be performed by suffixes, such as:

- Turning adjectives into adverbs:

  quick + -ly → quick**ly**   happy + -ly → happi**ly**

- Turning adjectives into verbs:

  modern + -ize → modern**ize**   simple + -ify → simpl**ify**

- Turning nouns into adjectives:

  hero + -ic → hero**ic**   child + -like → child**like**

The suffixes which have most to do with grammar are of a different kind. These are the word-endings called **inflections**, and they are described on p. 14.

Prefixes and suffixes together

A prefix and a suffix may both be used along with one base form:
  un-drink-able   bi-lingual-ism
Sometimes more than one prefix or suffix may be used in the same word:
  nation-al-iz-ation   un-re-turn-able
We can make quite lengthy words in English by combining prefixes and suffixes in this way. Scientific terms are often very long, for this reason, and people have even invented 'monster' words, using several prefixes and suffixes:
  de-oxy-ribo-nucle-ic
  anti-dis-establish-ment-arian-ism
When words have a string of elements in this way, it isn't usually possible to change their order. We cannot say:
  *re-un-turnable   *nation-iz-al-ation.

Activities

A Add a suffix

Here is a list of base forms and a list of suffixes. Work out which forms go with which, then write a sentence to show how the words could be used. Note that some base forms allow the use of different suffixes.

king   auction   lion   quick   help   simple   false
duck   pay   act   drain   puzzle   kind

-ify   -ess   -ly   -ness   -ling   -dom   -age
-ful   -hood   -ee   -or   -eer   -ment

B Correct the errors

This non-native speaker of English has failed to learn which suffixes go with which base forms. Make appropriate changes, by attaching the correct suffix to the base form, and use the correct word in a sentence.

1 ducklet   2 starvingness   3 mountainer   4 bookling   5 rapidness
6 violiner   7 singor   8 modernify   9 dukess   10 delightless

C Analyse word structure

- Group these words into those which consist simply of a base form and those which have one or more prefixes or suffixes.

- Put the base forms in one list, and in another list show the parts of the more complex words, as on the facing page.

- Choose five of the words which contain a prefix or suffix, and write short definitions of them. Then find another word which is made in the same way, and use it in a sentence. The first example is done for you.

> **rewrite** → re- + write 'to write something again', 'to revise'
> We have to **rethink** what we're doing tomorrow night.

1 large   5 chiefdom   9 cups   13 deforestation
2 rebuild   6 litre   10 supernatural 14 secretive
3 overwork   7 archbishop   11 finalist   15 surprising
4 quick   8 sadden   12 horse   16 undo

D Decode new words

Knowing your prefixes and suffixes can help you to work out what a word might mean, even if you have never seen it before. These words don't exist, but if they did, what would they mean?

1 extrastupidness   2 promulticrispsocracy   3 minihomeworkist
4 maxiwashify   5 superguitarster   6 antidefilthification

2 *Word endings*

One small group of suffixes can be used only at the one end of a word, after the other suffixes, if there are any. After *spoon*, we can add an *-s* ending and say *spoons*. After *jump* we can add an *-ed* ending and say *jumped*. Word endings like this are called **inflections**. Inflections don't have meanings like those of other suffixes. The job of an inflection is grammatical: it shows how a word is being used in a sentence.

Not all words can have inflections. If we take *The cat played on the log*, we can add *-s* endings to *cat* and *log* easily enough: *The cats played on the logs*. But we cannot add any endings to *the* or *on*: it doesn't sound right to say **ons the logs* or **thes cats*.

There are very few types of inflection in English, but each type is frequent. You'll find dozens of examples whenever you open a book (see p. 16). Inflections are best described in relation to the type of word they are attached to, so you'll find them again in the sections on nouns, verbs, adjectives, adverbs, and pronouns.

Inflections you can add to nouns

- One type of inflection shows that there is 'more than one' noun (**plural**). The usual ending is *-s*, as in *cats*, but there are also some irregular plurals, such as *mice* (see p. 74).

- Another inflection expresses the idea of 'belonging'. *The giraffe's neck* means 'the neck belonging to the giraffe'. This inflection is popularly called 'apostrophe s', but you will hear it more technically called the **genitive** inflection (see p. 82).

Inflections you can add to verbs

- The meaning of 'past time' is expressed by adding an inflection to a verb, as in *I walked* (see p. 114). The usual ending is *-ed*, but there are several irregular forms, such as *I ran* (not **I runned*) and *I said* (not **I sayed*).

- Another verb inflection expresses a meaning of 'action in progress' by adding an *-ing* ending, as in *I'm drinking* (see p. 116).

- Putting an *-s* ending after a verb shows that just one person – but not the speaker or the person you are talking to – is currently carrying out an action. In Standard English we say *I run*, *you run*, and *they run*, but *the giraffe runs* (see p. 104).

- You can add *n't* after certain verbs to express 'not': *they aren't* (see p. 110).

Inflections you can add to adjectives and adverbs

- You can add an *-er* or *-est* ending after some adjectives and adverbs to express comparison: *green*, *greener* ('more green'), *greenest* ('most green') (see p. 136).

Inflections you can add to pronouns

- Some pronouns change their form in different parts of the sentence. We do not say **I saw he* but *I saw him*. These unusual inflections are described on p. 128.

Activities

A Turn into Standard English

When we first began to learn language, we made lots of errors. Look at these child sentences, and identify which inflections are wrong or missing. Rewrite the sentences in adult Standard English.

1 Mummy goed in the garden.
2 I see daddy car.
3 I got the bestest one.
4 The mans bettern't do that.
5 Me don't like them mouses.
6 Liza jump over the wall.
7 You made it biggerer.
8 It go round and round.
9 Her got two leg.
10 I willn't go to bed.

B Use inflections

This extract from Arthur Ransome's *Swallows and Amazons* has been written out without any inflections. The words which have been changed are in brackets.

- Write out what the inflected forms should be. (Some of them are irregular.)

- Discuss what happens when you do not use inflections. Compare the effect with the sentences given in section C below.

Roger, [age] seven, and no [long] the [young] of the family, [run] in wide [zigzag], to and fro, across the steep field that [slope] up from the lake to Holly Howe, the farm where they [be] [stay] for part of the summer [holiday]. He [run] until he nearly [reach] the hedge on the other side of the field. Then he [turn] and [cross] the field again. Each crossing of the field [bring] him [near] to the farm. The wind [be] against [he], and he [be] [tack] up against it to the farm, where at the gate his patient mother [be] [await] [he].

C Analyse a pidgin

Here are some sentences from a pidgin English of West Africa, Kamtok, which does not use the inflections of Standard English. Identify which inflections are not being used, and discuss how Kamtok expresses the meaning in a different way.

The first column gives the spelling used by the person who wrote the language down. The second column spells the word in Standard English, but keeps the pidgin grammar. And the third 'translates' this grammar into Standard English.

Yam dia.	Yams dear.	Yams are dear.
Wi no wan wes wi banana.	We no want waste we banana.	We don't want to waste our bananas.
Di doa dohn opehn.	The door done open.	The door has just opened.
I di havehst manggo.	She do harvest mango.	She is harvesting mangoes.
A geht plehnti frehn.	I get plenty friend.	I have lots of friends.

Suffix-spotting

This extract from Terry Pratchett's *Reaper Man* (Chapter 1) shows how you will find suffixes scattered throughout a text. Look out for the following points:

- Some words contain two suffixes, as in *person-al-ity* and *chill-i-er*.

- Some words change their spelling or pronunciation when you add a suffix: for example, the *e* of *argue* is lost in the word *argument*.

- Some suffixes can be used for many words: the *-ed* ending, for example, is used in *floated*, *described*, *numbered*, and several other verbs. When many words in the language use an ending in the same way, we say that the inflection is **regular**.

- There are a number of words where the regular suffix is not used. In the extract, you'll find several verbs where the meaning of past time is not marked by an *-ed* ending. Instead, they use special forms, as in the case of *said* (from *say*) and *did* or *done* (from *do*). These are some of the **irregular** forms in English. *Has* is also irregular – we do not say **haves*. The most irregular verb of all is *to be*, which has such forms as *is*, *was*, *were*, and *been*, all used in the extract.

- There are also several examples of pronouns in their different forms. You will find both *they* and *them*, *he* and *him*. These are irregular also. No other words in the language change their shape in the way pronouns do.

Only regular suffixes are highlighted, in the extract below.

> *Three grey figures floated just above it. Exactly what they were can't be described in normal language. Some people might call them cherubs, although there was nothing rosy-cheeked about them. They might be numbered among those who see to it that gravity operates and that time stays separate from space. Call them auditors. Auditors of reality.*
>
> *They were in conversation without speaking. They didn't need to speak. They just changed reality so that they had spoken.*
>
> *One said, It has never happened before. Can it be done?*
>
> *One said, It will have to be done. There is a personality. Personalities come to an end. Only forces endure.*
>
> *It said this with a certain satisfaction.*
>
> *One said, Besides ... there have been irregularities. Where you get personality, you get irregularities. Well-known fact.*
>
> *One said, He has worked inefficiently?*
>
> *One said, No. We can't get him there.*
>
> *One said, That is the point. The word is him. Becoming a personality is inefficient. We don't want it to spread. Supposing gravity developed a personality? Supposing it decided to like people?*
>
> *One said, Got a crush on them, sort of thing?*
>
> *One said, in a voice that would have been even chillier if it was not already at absolute zero, No.*
>
> *One said, Sorry. Just my little joke.*

Activities

A Say what inflections do

This list gives some of the inflections used in the extract from *Reaper Man*. For each one, explain what its purpose is. The first example is done for you.

figures   The -s inflection shows that there's more than one figure.

1 float**ed**
2 can**'t**
3 irregularitie**s**
4 becom**ing**
5 chilli**er**
6 operate**s**

B Play a language game

- The aim is to make the longest word possible using a base form, prefixes, and suffixes (including inflections). The game is called 'Asterisk'.

- People play it in pairs, and take turns to start. Toss a coin to decide who goes first.

- If you are the first player, you think up a prefix. Your opponent then has to continue the word with a base form. You go next, adding a suffix. Your opponent goes next, adding another suffix. And so on. You write down each word that each player makes. All words must be real words in English (you will need a dictionary to check on uncertain examples).

- For each correct new word, you score a point. If the word is incorrect, you lose a point. If you cannot go, you say 'Pass'. Your opponent then takes your turn – and scores double points if successful. The game ends when neither you nor your opponent can think of a way of making the word longer.

- You can challenge your opponent if you think a word is not acceptable, by saying 'Asterisk'. If you are right, your opponent loses a point. (Similarly, your opponent can challenge you.)

Player A starts with a prefix, e.g. *dis-*.	A gains 1 point
Player B continues with a base form, e.g. *disapprove*.	B gains 1 point
Player A continues with *disapproving*.	A gains 1 point
Player B continues with *disapprovingness*.	
A challenges. It isn't in the dictionary.	B loses 1 point
Player A cannot go.	A loses 1 point
Player B recovers, with *disapprovingly*.	B gains 2 points
No further guesses.	
Game over. B wins, 2-1.	

3 *Compound words*

It is possible to have words which look quite complicated, but which do not have any prefixes or suffixes. This is usually because two base forms have been joined together. *Arm* is one base form. *Chair* is another. If we add *arm* to *chair* we get *armchair*. Words like this, which consist of more than one base form, are called **compound** words. There are thousands of compounds in English. In each case, a new word has been formed, with a new meaning: *armchair* means 'chair with arms'.

Here are some other compound words, along with their meaning:

chewing + gum → chewing-gum   'gum for chewing'
hand + made → hand-made   'made by hand'
washing + machine → washing machine   'machine for washing things'
scare + crow → scarecrow   'something that scares crows'
theatre + goer → theatre-goer   'someone who goes to the theatre'

You may not have seen a particular compound word before, but if you know the meaning of the component parts, you can usually guess what it might mean. A *stonebasher* is presumably a person or thing which bashes stones.

Note that some compounds are written without any space between the elements; some do have a space; and some are joined with a hyphen. Learning which form is correct is part of the task of learning to spell. But you will find that usage varies quite a bit: for example, all three forms *flower pot*, *flower-pot*, and *flowerpot* are used in print.

Compound words can sometimes be found with prefixes and suffixes. *Motor + bike* produces *motorbike*, and from here we could get *minimotorbike*. *Home + sick* produces *homesick*, and from here we could get *homesickness*.

Some unusual compounds

In each of the compound words listed above, the two elements are easy to identify, because each element can be used on its own as a separate word. But there are some words where one of these elements is not so easy to identify.

For example, in the 1990s, several words have been coined to talk about the new concepts arising out of the European Union, such as *Euromoney*, *Eurodollars*, and *Eurofighter*. *Euro-* is the first element, but it is not used on its own as a separate word: it is a shortened form of *European*. Its most famous use is probably in *EuroDisney*.

Here are some other words where one of the elements has been shortened:

bio- (= biological)   biodata   biotechnology
techno- (= technology)   technostress   technophobia
-athon (= marathon)   swimathon   readathon
-aholic (= alcoholic)   workaholic   computaholic

Activities

A Analyse meanings

Write a comment which expresses the meaning of ten of the following compounds.
The first two are done for you.

working party → a party which works
book-reviewer → someone who reviews books

1 bar-tender	6 window-cleaner	11 sleepwalker
2 landslide	7 punchbag	12 handwriting
3 popcorn	8 spending money	13 babysitter
4 haircut	9 hiding-place	14 homework
5 sightseeing	10 sewing machine	15 doorknob

B Provide definitions

Choose ten of these compound words, write a sentence explaining what each part of
the compound means, then define the whole word. Make a special note of cases
where the meaning of the whole word is very different from its parts.

1 bottleneck	6 gate-crasher	11 brainwashing
2 safety belt	7 living-room	12 lawn-mower
3 food poisoning	8 catcall	13 doghouse
4 dragonfly	9 turntable	14 waiting room
5 hay fever	10 handshake	15 cable car

C Explain new compounds

Here are some compound words for people, things, or processes which may not
exist yet. Write a sentence explaining what each one probably does.

1 bean-counter	6 iceberg-dweller
2 dream receiver	7 applause machine
3 translation box	8 eggkeeper
4 goldfish bar	9 frog-operator
5 bedhouse	10 measles remover

D Invent some compounds

Use the following base forms to make ten new compound words for people, things,
or processes. Take a base form from line A and put it in front of one from line B.
Then write a sentence to say what each invention does.

A: cheese   cornflakes   lemonade   tooth   jeans   beard   handkerchief
B: keeper   shed   goer   powder   machine   designer   taking   knife

Sentences

2 Sentences

The main aim of grammar is to describe the way the **sentences** of a language are constructed. A sentence is the chief means we have of organizing our thoughts so that they make sense, both to ourselves and to others, in speech and in writing.

4 *What is a sentence?*

Think of a sentence as a unit of language which makes sense. You construct sentences by using the rules of grammar. That is what grammar is for: to make sentences.

When you construct sentences, there are three important points to bear in mind.

Sentences need to be complete

If a string of words is to count as a sentence, it must be able to stand by itself, and feel finished. These word strings cannot be sentences, because we feel that something important is missing:

> the fast ferry   bigger than   which of all the books
> because Mary said   can be done   so

On the other hand, nothing seems to be missing in these word strings:

> The fast ferry is bigger than the slow ferry.
> I believe the job can be done because Mary said so.

What do we need to make a sentence feel complete? The answer is on p. 30.

Sentences need to be grammatical

The words in a sentence can appear only in certain patterns, and these patterns reflect the rules of grammar. Some rules control the order in which the words appear. Others control the endings certain words have (see p. 14). If a sentence is constructed according to these rules, we call it **grammatical**. Grammatical sentences feel natural and acceptable. If a sentence breaks the rules, we call it **ungrammatical**. Ungrammatical sentences feel awkward and un-English.

All the sentences on this page so far are grammatical. Here are some ungrammatical ones. Say them to yourself, and check that they do not sound right.

> *The a car saw man.   *We might didn't not of gone.
> *The clocks is be ready.   *What and why did she go?

When you find an ungrammatical sentence, you can mark it with an asterisk, as here, to show that it is not an acceptable part of English grammar.

Sentences can be any length

Most sentences consist of several words, but it is possible to have a sentence which is just one word long, such as *Sorry!* Others can be hundreds of words long. Indeed, if you imagine a sentence beginning *I saw a cat and a dog and a car ...*, it could go on for ever! However, if sentences get too long, it can be difficult to work out what is being said. Most of the sentences in this book are less than 20 words in length.

Activities

A Find the sentences

Look at these strings of words, and decide which are sentences (✓) and which are not (✗). Pay attention only to how complete they feel, because there are no capital letters or punctuation marks to help you. When you've decided on the sentences, write them out with capital letters and punctuation.

1 the journey to France took three hours
2 a new car
3 on Thursday
4 slow down
5 because it had been raining for days
6 will be travelling
7 where's the salt
8 she put her book
9 if you like
10 we bought some ice cream when we were in town

B Make everything grammatical

Look at this list of sentences. Some of them are grammatical and some are ungrammatical, but there are no asterisks to tell you which is which. Rewrite the ungrammatical sentences to make them grammatical. (Note that there may be more than one way of doing this.)

1 A book red is on the table.
2 Everyone liked the clowns.
3 I could may go to town tomorrow.
4 Where can we buy a newspaper?
5 He cut herself with a piece of glass.
6 I had a drink because thirsty was I.
7 The answer knows who?
8 The picture fell off the wall.
9 We got up at six o'clock.
10 They ran home fastly.

C Carry out a survey of sentence length

1 Collect a range of different written texts, such as a newspaper, a novel, a leaflet, a children's story, and a science textbook, and carry out a survey of the average sentence length in each.

   • Count the number of words in the first ten sentences, and decide on the average length. See which type of text uses the longest sentences.

   • Are there any instances where you begin to lose the meaning because the sentences are too long? Try rewriting these long sentences as a series of shorter sentences.

2 Find some assignments of your own, and work out your average sentence length. How does it compare with other people's? Does it vary in different subjects? Are your sentences ever too long?

3 If a sentence contains a list of points, or a set of examples, it can become quite long yet still be easy to understand. Find two examples in the last paragraph of the facing page. Collect some other examples of sentences over 20 words in length, and discuss why they are so long.

Sentences in writing and in speech

In writing, a capital letter can help to show where a sentence begins. A punctuation mark can help to show where it ends. The full-stop, question mark, and exclamation mark are the chief ways of signalling that a sentence is finished.

> The disaster wiped out the dinosaurs.   That's ridiculous!
> Why did the chicken cross the road?

By contrast, a dash (–) or three dots (. . .) is often used to show that a sentence is unfinished.

> 'It was . . . It was . . .' Smith's head fell forward. He was dead.

But beware: not all written sentences have punctuation marks. In headlines, road signs, and public notices, there may be no punctuation at all (see p. 28).

In speech, the end of a sentence is often signalled by the tune and rhythm of the voice, and by the use of a pause. But it is always much more difficult to identify sentences in speech, especially when people are chatting casually. Speakers loosely string several constructions into a long chain, linking them with such words as *and*. Here's an extract from a story which went on and on for nearly three minutes! (The main pauses are shown by dashes.)

> *so I was walking along the road – and I saw this man looking into a hole – and he was a funny-looking chap – but he wasn't doing any harm – and so as I went past I looked down this hole – and right at the bottom there was a sort of red shape . . .*

Different rules

The rules which govern the way we write English sentences are not always the same as those which govern the way we speak them. For example, *ain't* is widely used in casual speech, all over the world, but it is considered totally unacceptable in most kinds of writing. And in speech, people say things like:

> The car went past the shop – you know, the shop in Smith Street.

because they are 'thinking on their feet', sorting out their thoughts while they speak. In careful writing, we have time to organize our ideas, so this sentence would probably appear as:

> The car went past the shop in Smith Street.

English grammars usually describe the sentence patterns of Standard English (see p. 6), and if a sentence has an asterisk in this book, it means that the construction is not grammatical in Standard English. But take care: the sentence may be perfectly grammatical in some other dialect. The rules of grammar are not always the same, as we move around the English-speaking world. For example, Americans often say *gotten* where British people would say *got. They've gotten a boat* is a grammatical sentence in American English, but it is ungrammatical in British English.

Activities

A Turn speech into writing

Here are some sentences which are often found in casual spoken English. Turn them into a form which would be more suitable for careful writing.

1 The customer ain't interested.
2 The screen didn't show no picture.
3 They bought a whatsit – a spanner.
4 Mind you, I was expecting trouble.
5 He's a very very very nice man.
6 Here's the play what I wrote.
7 There was all this dirt in the road.
8 They looked out the window.
9 The hotel was bleedin' expensive.
10 The manager should sort of tell everyone.

B Turn a speech into writing

Here is the opening of an after-dinner speech. The transcription shows only the places where the speaker paused. There are no capital letters to show the beginning of a sentence, and no punctuation marks to show the end.

- Write out each sentence on a separate line, giving it a capital letter and an appropriate ending mark. (Beware: in one place there is an unfinished sentence.)

- Look out for any other punctuation changes you may need to make.

i'm delighted to be here with you this evening – it's many years since i was last in liverpool – on that occasion i'm told i was in a push-chair and more interested in a penny lollipop than in my surroundings – funnily enough when i arrived today the first person i met was a man selling lollipops – i had to buy one of course – in fact i bought two because – but before i go into that let me ask you a question – how much do you think a modern penny lollipop costs – it certainly isn't a penny any more – would it be 10p – would you pay 20p pehaps – well let me tell you that i paid 50p for a lollipop that was no bigger than a 50p piece – it's absolutely incredible –

C Discuss regional dialects and Standard English

Here are some sentences taken from regional dialects of English (e.g. Scots, Lancashire, Liverpool, American).

- Write them out as they might appear in Standard British English.

- In a group, discuss which dialects they could belong to. (Note that some are found in several dialects.) Are any of the dialect features used where you live?

1 They've wrote me three letters.
2 I just ignores people like that.
3 You're going, isn't it?
4 How are y'all feeling today?
5 We didnae think o' that.
6 We couldn't see nowt.
7 Who is it you'll be wanting?
8 Can I give youse a lift?
9 Why they do that?
10 We was walking down the road.

5 *Types of sentence*

It is obvious, as we look through the pages of a novel, or a daily newspaper, that there must be a very large number of grammatical sentence patterns in English. What is less obvious is that these can be grouped into two main types, on the basis of whether they are formed in a **regular** or **irregular** way. This book will chiefly deal with the structure of regular sentences. Irregular sentences are described on p. 28.

Regular sentences

Most of the sentences in English are constructed in a regular way. All the sentences in this book, apart from the headings and a few of the examples, are of this type. Essentially, they are sentences which can be broken down into a **limited pattern of elements**, such as these:

My friend	has dropped	a book	on her big toe.
I	gave	the keys	to Luke.
Jemima	went	to town	yesterday.

These limited patterns of elements are called **clauses**. We shall see what can be a clause, and what to call its elements, on p. 30.

Simple and multiple sentences

Look at the difference between these two sentences:

A book fell on John's toe.
A book fell on John's toe and a book fell on Janet's toe.

The same clause patterns turn up twice in the second sentence. Indeed, it is possible to imagine a sentence where this clause pattern is used repeatedly, with lots of books falling on lots of toes, each clause being joined to the next by a linking word, such as *and*.

So, sentences may consist of just one clause, or of more than one clause. A one-clause sentence is called a **simple sentence**. A sentence which can be immediately analysed into more than one clause is called a **multiple sentence**. The difference can be summarized in a diagram.

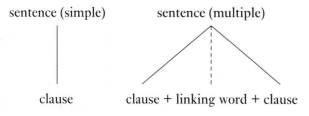

sentence (simple)   sentence (multiple)

clause   clause + linking word + clause

Activities

A Find the clause elements

Look at these regular sentences. Each consists of just one clause. Write each clause out with breaks to show the elements it contains. The first one is done for you.

1 My aunt Emma bought a new car. → My aunt Emma / bought / a new car.
2 I like bananas.
3 The car went to the garage today.
4 We asked the shopkeeper for some change.
5 Who paid the bill?
6 Leave the key on the table.
7 We travelled on foot in the rain up the mountain.
8 In the garden I saw a huge coloured slide.
9 Last year our team won the cup.
10 A pair of large eyes peered over the fence.

B Turn multiple into simple

Here is a passage containing several multiple sentences. Rewrite the passage, leaving out the linking words so that there are only simple sentences left. In a group, discuss the differences you feel between the two styles.

> *I went to town because the weather had turned nasty and I wanted a new coat. The train was late and I had to wait for nearly an hour. I forget the reason, but I think there had been an accident somewhere. Eventually I got to the shops, but half of them were closed. I'd forgotten that it was early-closing day. One shop had some nice coats, but they weren't much use to me because they were too expensive.*

C Turn simple into multiple

In this extract from Len Deighton's *The Billion Dollar Brain*, the words linking some of the clauses have been taken out, so there are only simple sentences left.

- Form a small group. Each member rewrites the passage with some linking words (e.g. and, but, when). Then compare your new versions.

- Discuss the different effects. How does the passage sound if you keep the sentences short? If you can get hold of Deighton's book, see what he does himself.

> *I was the sole passenger. I left New York in Midwinter's Jetstar. The weather bureau was predicting light rain and snow flurries. The cirrus was thickening. Over San Antonio, Texas, three and a half hours later the night was crystal clear. The landscape was green. The trees were dense with leaves. The air clung like a warm face-cloth. Men moved in the leisurely evening warmth like alligators across a mud-flat.*

Irregular sentences

Some sentences are not constructed in a regular way. They make use of unusual patterns which cannot be clearly analysed into a sequence of clause elements, as regular sentences can. There are only a few types of irregular sentence, but instances of each type are frequently used in daily life – and everyday conversation, in particular, makes great use of them.

Irregular sentences are also common in notices, headlines, labels, and other kinds of written language where a message is presented as a 'block' of text.

> For Sale   No Smoking   THE TIMES   WAY OUT

These sentences are not usually given any punctuation, because the place where they are used (such as on a notice board) makes it obvious when they have ended.

Some common types of irregular sentence

- Useful **formulas** for everyday social situations.

  > Hello!   Thanks.   Cheers!   How do?
  > Nice day!   All aboard!   Taxi!   Oh for a Coke!

- Emotional noises (or **interjections**).

  > Eh?   Hey!   Tut-tut.   Yuk!   Ow!   Shhh!

- Proverbs or short, punchy sayings (or **aphorisms**).

  > Easy come, easy go.   Least said, soonest mended.

Frozen sentences

Some irregular sentences have to be learned as a whole, because their parts cannot be altered. *God save the Queen!* is a good example. Although this looks as if it is a regular sentence, in fact it is not, because the string of words cannot be changed according to the normal rules of grammar. Unless we are deliberately trying to be funny, we do not say:

> God might save the Queen!   God hasn't been saving the Queen!

At first sight, *God save the Queen* looks like the regular sentence *Gonzo saved his money*. But you can carry out a grammar experiment to show that the two are different. You **can** use the normal rules of grammar to alter the *Gonzo* sentence:

> Gonzo might save his money.   Gonzo hasn't been saving his money.

This proves that *Gonzo saved his money* is a regular sentence.

A vivid way of describing sentences like *God save the Queen!* is to say that their structure is 'frozen solid'. Other frozen sentences are:

> Lord forbid!   How come?   How do you do? (as a greeting)

It is difficult to alter these sentences without them becoming ungrammatical:

> *Lord is forbidding!   *How came?   *How don't you do?

Activities

A Classify irregular sentences

Look at these sentences, and decide which are social formulas, interjections, and aphorisms. – *short pithy statement or Maxim*

1 Wow!
2 Pleased to meet you.
3 Once bitten, twice shy.
4 Merry Christmas!
5 How are you?
6 Love me, love my dog.
7 'Bye.
8 No homework, no TV.
9 Down with Smith!
10 Yeah.
11 Checkmate.
12 Uh-huh.
13 Good morning.
14 So far, so good.
15 Boo!
16 Happy Birthday.
17 Goal!
18 No sooner said than done.
19 Cheers!
20 Ouch!

B Explain frozen sentences

Here are some sentences which look as if they are regular, but in fact they are irregular. Imagine you have to teach them to a Martian. Write a sentence explaining what each one means and when you would use it.

1 Don't mention it.
2 Heaven help us!
3 See you!
4 Long live the Republic!
5 Hands up!
6 I beg your pardon.
7 Too many cooks spoil the broth.
8 Bless you!
9 May the Force be with you!
10 Watch it!

C Carry out an irregular sentence survey

- Start an irregular sentence collection. As you walk round the school, make a note of any irregular sentences you see. Compare your list with someone else's.

- Bring in a copy of your favourite magazine, and do a sentence analysis of the cover. List all the irregular sentences you find. Are there any regular sentences there at all?

D Write a sketch

Write a sketch using as few regular sentences as possible. Make the conversation sound as natural as you can. It might start like this:

A: Hello.
B: Hi.
A: How are things?
B: Oh for a banana!
A: No sooner said, than done.
B: Cheers!
A: Easy come, easy go! . . .

Now perform your sketch in front of the class.

6 *The parts of a clause*

All clauses are made up out of **elements**, each expressing a particular kind of meaning. There are just five types of clause element. All appear in this sentence:

> The teacher / called / Jill / a genius / twice.

- The first element in this sentence is the **subject** (usually abbreviated as **S**). The chief job of the subject is to identify the topic of the clause – what the clause is going to be about. In this sentence, we are introduced to a teacher; the rest of the sentence tells us what the teacher did.

- The second element is the **verb (V)**. The verb is the most important element in the clause. It can express a wide range of meanings, such as actions, sensations, or states of being. The verbs so far used on this page include *express*, *appear*, *abbreviate*, *identify*, *tell* and *be*.

- The third element is the **object (O)**. Objects identify who or what has been directly affected by the verb's action. In the above sentence, it is Jill who has been called the genius. Here are some other objects: *I kicked __the ball__. We saw __the moon__.*

- The fourth element is the **complement (C)**. The job of the complement is to give extra information about the subject or object. In the above sentence, *a genius* adds something extra to the meaning of *Jill*. Jill *is* a genius, says the teacher.

- The fifth element is the **adverbial (A)**. Adverbials usually add information about the situation, telling us when an action took place, or where, or how. In the above sentence, *twice* tells us how often the action of calling took place. To see some other adverbial meanings, try replacing *twice* by *yesterday* or *in the garden*.

Long and short elements

The number of words belonging to a clause element varies greatly. Each element could be as short as one word; some could be quite long strings of words. Here are clauses containing one-word elements and two-word elements.

S	V	O	C	A
She	called	her	it	twice.
The teacher	was calling	my sister	a genius	last week.

You can experiment with much longer elements. Try replacing *The teacher* with *The foreign-looking student from the corner house*. Or *last week* by *at the top of the school clock tower*. Or *was calling* by *didn't want to have to keep on calling*. Expand all the elements at the same time and you can end up with a monster sentence:

The foreign-looking student from the corner house / didn't want to have to keep on calling / my tall, 16-year-old, blonde, blue-eyed friend from Scotland / a really clever and interesting person / at the top of the school clock tower.

Activities

A Combine elements into clauses

Here is a collection of possible clause elements. Arrange them in various ways to
make ten clauses of different lengths. Make sure that each clause makes sense as a
sentence, and has all the elements it needs to be grammatical. Then try labelling the
elements as S, V, C, O or A.

my uncle Ernie	an enthusiastic stamp–collector	several times
called	under an umbrella	a wise old owl
your aunt Jane	our next-door neighbour	prodded
didn't visit	an extremely ignorant so-and-so	happily
last Monday	was kissing	with a bowl of soup
in the garden	our head teacher	saw

B Identify clause elements

Write out these one-clause sentences, and identify the different clause elements in
each one. The first one is done for you. (Beware: the elements won't always be in
the same order as those on the facing page.)

1 I asked her twice. → I / asked / her / twice.
                  S   V   O   A
2 Everyone blames me!
3 Michael is playing a violin.
4 Michael is playing a violin very badly.
5 We painted the bus mauve.
6 Put the book on the table right now.
7 The driver quickly stopped the bulldozer.
8 My mate has been dancing in the fountain.
9 Sometimes the train has an extra carriage.
10 My friend called the horror film a load of rubbish.

- Which elements turn up (a) in every sentence? (b) in most sentences?

- Which elements did you find (a) easiest to spot? (b) most difficult to spot?

C Experiment with longer sentences

Take these sentences and expand each clause element to make monster sentences.
Compare your results with someone else's.

1 We like crisps.   2 I go home tomorrow.
3 I declared Mary the winner.   4 In cartoons, mice chase cats.

Which elements did you find (a) easiest to expand, (b) most difficult to expand?

7 *Making clause patterns*

The five clause elements combine into a very small number of patterns to make simple sentences. There are dozens of possible permutations, but only a few are actually allowed in Standard English grammar. For example, there are many simple sentences of the form **SVO** or **VSA**:

The doctor / examined / the patient.　Is / she / outside?
　S　　　　V　　　　O　　　　　V　　S　　A

But there are no simple sentences of the form **VOS** or **SOV**:

*Examined / the patient / the doctor　　*The doctor / the patient / examined.
　V　　　　O　　　　S　　　　　　　　S　　　　O　　　　V

However, you will sometimes find these unusual word orders in poetry or regional dialects.

The basic clause patterns

There are seven basic clause patterns in English.

TYPE	EXAMPLE
● S + V	Hilary yawned.
● S + V + O	Hilary / opened /the door.
● S + V + C	Hilary / was / ready.
● S + V + A	Hilary / lived / in London.
● S + V + O + O	Hilary / gave / me / a pen.
● S + V + O + C	Hilary / got / my shoes / wet.
● S + V + O + A	Hilary / put / the box / on the table.

Changing the order

There are just a few ways to change the order of elements in a clause. For example, we can take any of the above patterns, and turn the statements into questions by putting a special type of verb in front of the subject (see p. 110). So:

Hilary opened the door can become Did Hilary open the door?
　S　　V　　　O　　　　　　　　V　　S　　　　O

You can also sometimes make a sentence more emphatic by taking an element which normally occurs towards the end, and putting it at the beginning:

Hilary / put / the box / on the table can become
　S　　V　　O　　　A

On the table / Hilary / put / the box.
　A　　　　S　　V　　O

Activities

A Make sentences grammatical

Rewrite the order of clause elements to make these sentences grammatical, like this:

*Examined the patient the doctor. → The doctor examined the patient.

1 *Their shoes got wet the children.
2 *Opened I suddenly the door.
3 *Jim in New York was living.
4 *A pen me gave Anne.
5 *Travelled we on Thursday to Paris.

B Identify clause patterns

Look at these sentences and decide which clause pattern they follow. There are two examples of each type. Draw lines between the clause elements and label them.

1 The audience applauded.
2 We went to Blackpool.
3 I kicked the ball.
4 She asked me a question.
5 The foul was obvious.
6 I'll wash the dishes tomorrow.
7 Mary called me a twit.
8 I love you.
9 John gave them the message.
10 Everyone's staring.
11 The game finished at 12.
12 You're a fine specimen.
13 They elected Smith president.
14 I've walked the dog today.

C Explain unusual clause patterns

● Here are some unusual patterns. See if you can write the clauses out with the elements in their normal order. Then discuss in a group why the writer might have chosen the unusual order.

1 Ten thousand saw I at a glance (Wordsworth)
2 With this ring, I thee wed (*Book of Common Prayer*)
3 Rude am I in my speech (Shakespeare)
4 Round many western islands have I been (Keats)
5 Strong with the Force you are (Yoda, in *Return of the Jedi*)

● Many unexpected word orders are to be found in poetry. Why is this?

D Create a clause story

Make up a clause story, using each of the clause patterns. Try to fit them all around a theme, such as a favourite television programme. Use the examples on the facing page to help you, but try to make your sentences as different as possible. Your clause story might begin like this:

Batman groaned. (SV)   He opened his eyes. (SVO)
His head was very sore. (SVC)   . . .

8 *The verb*

The verb element in a clause plays a central role in clause structure. It can hardly ever be left out, without the clause becoming ungrammatical. We can see this by playing with the following four-element clause:

That old farmer / drinks / beer / by the bucketful.
     <u>S</u>   <u>V</u>   <u>O</u>   <u>A</u>

- We can leave out the adverbial, and still have a grammatical clause: *That old farmer / drinks / beer.*

- We can leave out the object, and still have a grammatical clause: *That old farmer / drinks / by the bucketful.*

- When talking very casually, we can leave out the subject, and still have a grammatical clause: *Drinks / beer / by the bucketful* – nodding in the farmer's direction. (But beware: it can be dangerous to leave out the subject in writing, because you cannot use activities like head-nodding to tell your reader who is carrying out an action.)

- However, we cannot leave out the verb, and still have a grammatical clause: **That old farmer / beer / by the bucketful.*

You can even have clauses which consist *only* of a verb: *Drink! Run! Stop!* These are commands, and they form part of an important class of sentences in English (see p. 62).

What can be a V?

The V element in a clause can be quite long and complex, but it usually consists of only two or three words, and often it has only one word in it. The following **SV** (Subject + Verb) clauses show some of the possibilities:

They   jumped.
They   were jumping.
They   weren't jumping.
They   have been jumping.
They   might have been jumping.
They   mightn't have been jumping.

Words like *jump*, *were*, *might*, *have*, and *been* are all verbs, but of two different kinds. *Jump* is obviously the word with most meaning, so it is called the **main verb**. The others all help to express further aspects of the meaning of *jump* – when the jumping took place, or whether it took place at all. They are therefore called 'helping verbs' or, more technically, **auxiliary verbs**. We shall look at these types of verb more closely on p. 110.

Activities

A Complete the clauses

Here are some clauses where the verb elements have been left out. Make the clauses grammatical by inserting suitable main verbs. Use auxiliary verbs (e.g. *can*, *is*, *have*), if you need them.

1 *She out of the house into the garden.
2 *Those rabbits very quickly.
3 *Another customer a tomato.
4 *John some help, please.
5 *Although I a coat, I cold.
6 *I Paris last year.

B Build new clauses

Choose five verbs, and build up clauses by adding one element at a time, like this:

> Come.
> Come here.
> The tourists come here.
> The tourists come here every summer.

Choose your verbs from this list: *eat, run, jump, go, help, stop, imagine, escape, concentrate.*

C Distinguish the verbs

Here is an extract from Charles Grant's *Whirlwind*, one of *The X Files*, where all the V elements have been highlighted. Copy these elements into a table, putting the main verbs in one column and any auxiliary verbs in another. Ignore any words which separate an auxiliary from its main verb. Your table should look like this:

AUXILIARY VERBS	MAIN VERBS
	imagine
had	mentioned

Imagine, Mulder **said**, a group of men, extremely devout men, **confined** for so long in a single room. The kiva. *Imagine*, as he **had** already **mentioned** to Scully, the energy they **must create** and **radiate** as they **perform** the rituals **required** of their faith. **Suppose**, then, there are moments during that time when the energy **can** no longer **be confined**, but its excess **escapes** through the hole in the ceiling. It **can dissipate**. Maybe someone nearby feels a little discomfort, but nothing more. They **might blame** it on the wind.

But **suppose**, just **suppose**, it **doesn't scatter**. **Suppose** it **gathers** instead. **Suppose** it **concentrates**.

Suppose the earliest Konochine **knew** this. They **would** also **know** that such a concentration **would be** potentially dangerous. So they **come** to the valley within the Wall from wherever they **had been**, and **make** it their home.

Controlling the clause

Your choice of verb largely controls which other elements you can have in a clause. Once you have 'picked' a verb, certain other things are going to happen.

- If you pick *go*, you can stop the clause there, without fear of being ungrammatical:

> That farmer / is going.
> <u>S</u>   <u>V</u>

Verbs of this type, which can be used without an object, are called **intransitive verbs**. Other common intransitive verbs are *fall*, *wait*, *die*, and *lie*. Try to replace *going* in the above sentence with *falling*, *waiting*, etc. You will find that the sentence still feels grammatical.

- If you pick *find*, another clause element has to follow. We cannot say: **That farmer / is finding*. It has to be 'finding something', with an object present:

> That farmer / is finding / his drink.
> <u>S</u>   <u>V</u>   <u>O</u>

Verbs which require an object are called **transitive verbs**. Other common transitive verbs are *carry*, *like*, *get*, and *make*. These verbs will all replace *find* – but they won't replace *go* in the previous paragraph.

Some verbs demand other elements. For example, if you pick *put*, **two** clause elements have to follow. We cannot say **That farmer / is putting*. It has to be 'putting something somewhere', with an object and an adverbial present:

> That farmer / is putting / his drink / on the table.
> <u>S</u>   <u>V</u>   <u>O</u>   <u>A</u>

Verbs with two uses

Watch out for those verbs which can be used in more than one way. *Eat* and *drink*, for example, can be used either as a transitive verb or as an intransitive verb. The sentences sound complete, whichever pattern is used.

INTRANSITIVE	TRANSITIVE
They're eating.	They're eating dinner.
They're drinking.	They're drinking some water.

Pay special attention to verbs which change their meaning when they switch from transitive to intransitive, or vice versa. Here are some of them:

TRANSITIVE	INTRANSITIVE
She's expecting a reply.	She's expecting.
I'm running a bath.	I'm running.
John is working wonders.	John is working.

Activities

A Correct the clauses

In these clauses, a non-native speaker hasn't understood the difference between transitive and intransitive verbs. Write out correct versions.

1 *They are going the bus.
2 *I am enjoying.
3 *That apple tree has died a disease.
4 *Will you wait the bus?
5 *The porter is carrying on a trolley.
6 *Will you find for me?
7 *The moon is rising the mountain.
8 *She's appearing the stage next week.
9 *Do you require?
10 *I'm using now.

B Decide about transitive and intransitive

Some clauses in this list have transitive verbs; some have intransitive verbs. Decide which is which, and label them with a T (transitive) or an I (intransitive). (Beware: some of the intransitive verbs in this list are not the last word in the clause.)

1 The shop made an excellent profit.
2 It's falling.
3 What's happening?
4 They have measles.
5 I need a new computer.
6 The horses are coming round the corner.
7 It doesn't matter.
8 She kicked the ball over the roof.
9 We can abolish all forms of pollution.
10 The train will arrive in five minutes.

C Change the meaning

This group of sentences all contain a transitive verb. (Note that the main verbs in examples 5, 8, and 10 contain two words: see p. 112 for more about these.) Leave out the objects to make a new sentence with an intransitive verb. Think what this new sentence could mean, and add some helpful context, like this:

> She's expecting a reply. → She's expecting (a baby).
> They're changing some money. → They're changing (on the beach).

1 John dropped the vase.
2 The cafe has closed its windows.
3 The neighbours have moved their car.
4 You've washed the dishes.
5 You've thrown up the chance.
6 Will you mind the dog?
7 Mary passed the butter.
8 Fred passed out the tickets.
9 Do you believe him?
10 Emma and Ian made up a story.

9 *The subject*

The subject is the most important element of the clause, apart from the verb. As its name suggests, its chief job is to tell you what the subject-matter, or topic, of the clause is going to be. When you know the subject, you know what the clause is talking about.

Imagine you are watching an awards programme on television. The presenter opens an envelope and says *The runner-up . . .* – then pauses dramatically, before carrying on. You've now heard the subject, so you know what the clause is going to be about: the runner-up, not the winner. Of course, a subject without the rest of the clause doesn't tell you very much – but it's a good start.

Finding the topic

Some clauses have a subject which tells you immediately what the topic is. Others make you look for it somewhere else.

- In *A car raced around the track*, you can tell immediately what the topic of this clause is: the subject is *a car*.

- However, imagine the next part of this story: *It crashed into a wall*. What is the subject here? The word *It*. And what does *It* refer to? *The car*, mentioned in the previous sentence.

There are many clauses like this, where the topic is not immediately clear. This is because the subject is a word which is referring back to something already mentioned in an earlier sentence.

Why does English do this? Think what would happen if it didn't. We would have to tell stories like this:

The car raced around the track. The car crashed into a wall. The car turned over twice. The car was badly damaged. In fact, the car was nearly a write-off.

Repeating the same subject all the time is cumbersome and boring. A word like *it* helps us to tell a story more quickly and efficiently.

The car raced around the track. It crashed into a wall. It turned over twice. It was badly damaged. In fact, it was nearly a write-off.

Of course, even this style would get boring if it was used all the time. Good story-telling switches between the two methods, and adds further variations, such as this:

The car raced around the track. It crashed into a wall, and turned over twice. The car was badly damaged. In fact, it was nearly a write-off.

Using *the car* in the third sentence is important. If the story-teller had used *it*, you might have wondered whether it was the car or the wall which was badly damaged.

Activities

A Remove the ambiguity

Look at these sequences of sentences. Something is wrong with the subject in each of the second sentences. An ambiguity or confusion has crept in. Rewrite the sentences to solve the problem.

1 The dog was chasing the cat. It was very angry.
2 John gave Jim a fiver. He was wearing a red tie at the time.
3 I bought some clothes and three tapes. They were quite a price.
4 Mary asked Anne to give the card to Jill. She was in a good mood that day.

B Find the missing subject

Each of these sentences contains two clauses. The subject of the second clause has been left out, because it's not needed – you can carry over the meaning of the subject from the first clause.

- Underline the subject of the first clause.

- Put an insert mark ($\wedge$) where the second subject has been left out.

1 Julie climbed the mountain and saw a marvellous sunrise.
2 The children saw a clown and had their pictures taken.
3 The box fell off the shelf and landed on the floor.
4 The plant was already three metres high and was growing larger.

C Avoid unnecessary repetition

Here is an extract from Grant Naylor's *Red Dwarf* sequel, *Better than Life*, but all the subjects have been written out in full (they are in bold type). The passage has become very repetitive and awkward. In a group, rewrite it to be more like the original text.

- You'll need to work out which subjects can be replaced by *it* or *he*.

- In two cases, it is more natural to leave out the subject. Decide which these are.

> *The planet was close now. The planet occupied almost half of Rimmer's navicomp screen, and the planet was growing steadily in size as the planet thundered towards them.*
>
> *Lister screwed up the empty sixth can of lager and Lister threw it across the room at the wastebin. The empty sixth can of lager hit the rim and the empty sixth can of lager clattered on the floor. ...*
>
> *Lister flicked the missile launch to manual. The firing pad lurched forward from the flatbed scanner, and Lister nestled his nose into the bifocal viewer. Heat prickled his arms and his forehead. Lister lined up the crosswires on the sun around which the cue planet spun. Lister shifted his legs until Lister felt his centre of balance.*

How can you tell what a subject is?

- The subject is usually the element which performs the action expressed by the verb:

  The cat saw the dog.   **The cow** jumped over the moon.

- If the sentence is a statement, the subject usually appears before the verb:

  Rain fell all day long.   **The bonfire** glowed in the dark.

The subject is usually the very first element in a clause. But take care: it is possible to emphasize another clause element by putting it before the subject:

    Yesterday, **rain** fell all day long.   In the dark, **the bonfire** glowed.

- If the sentence is a question, the subject appears after the opening verb:

  Are **you** going far?   Did **the bonfire** glow in the dark?

- If the subject is a pronoun referring to a person, it may have a distinct **subjective** form. We say *I, he, she, we,* and *they.* In other parts of the clause, these words change to *me, him, her, us,* and *them.*

  I saw John.   John saw **me**.
  She gave it to Mary.   Mary gave it to **her**.

Notice that *you* and *it* do not change their form, as they move around the clause. We say both *You saw John* and *John saw you.*

- You can also sometimes identify the subject of a clause by showing how it controls the verb: this interesting feature is described on p. 52.

What can be a subject?

- A subject can be just a single noun:
  Shirley shook her head.   **Stratford** is a popular spot.

- More commonly, subjects can be a string of words based on a noun (a **noun phrase**):
  The train was late.   **All the people** were wearing black hats.

- You can also have a string of nouns working together as a list:
  The crisps, cheese, and ice-cream are on the table.
  Note that this is not a sequence of three subjects, but a single, complex subject. There is only one subject per clause.

- Words like *it,* which refer back to nouns, are called **pronouns** (see p. 128). Pronouns are the most frequently occurring subjects in everyday speech. *I,* the pronoun which refers to the speaker, is one of the commonest words in conversational English.

Activities

A Find the subject

Write out these sentences, and underline the subject. Look out for sentences with more than one clause, where there is a subject in each.

1 The car cost nearly 9 thousand.
2 The frying pan fell on the floor.
3 I like bananas.
4 She slowly opened the door.
5 Everybody went to the party.
6 Cheese and crisps are on sale.
7 I like bananas but Joe doesn't.
8 A very wide range of CDs is on sale.
9 You've met my rotweiler?
10 We have a puncture and the car's got no petrol.

B Answer the question

In the following examples, the subject of the first sentence is a question word. Underline it, and prove that the answer to the question is a subject by showing the rest of its sentence, like this. (Beware No. 5, where you have to do something else as well.)

> Who went to town? → John.   (went to town)

1 Who made that noise?   Cardew.
2 What was in the hole?   A pool of water.
3 Which is the way to Upton?   That way.
4 What's in the shadows?   Dracula.
5 Who likes ice cream?   Me.

C Put the subject first

In these sentences the subject is not the first element in the clause.

- Find where it is, and underline it.

- Rewrite each sentence so that the subject *is* the first element in the clause, like this:

> Can you pay for my ticket? → You can pay for my ticket.

1 Later, two people bought copies.
2 Are the children fast asleep?
3 Have you heard the latest news?
4 On Friday the weather was awful.
5 Hardly had she left when it started to rain.
6 Unfortunately, some of the apples were bad.
7 Of course we'll visit you.
8 Were Joan and Margaret at the club?
9 As a matter of fact, I was one of the first to arrive.
10 After a terrible journey across the mountain, they arrived in the camp.

10 *The object*

The object in a clause tells you who or what has been directly affected by the action of the verb. It usually comes immediately after the subject and verb. SVO (Subject–Verb–Object) is the basic clause pattern in English.

Clauses with one object

In most clauses, there is just one object.

The little boy smashed **a window**.   The referee kicked **the ball**.
S   V   O   S   V   O

Here, the window has undoubtedly been affected by the action of smashing, and the ball by the action of kicking. It is the window which has been smashed – not the little boy. And it is the ball which has been kicked – not the referee. (The little boy and the referee are subjects, the persons doing the action (see p. 38).)

In the following clauses, the verbs are not really actions, but their meaning affects the object in a similar way.

I saw **the car**.   The table has **four legs**.
S V   O   S   V   O

The car is what has been seen. The four legs are what the table has got.

What can be an object?

- As with subjects, an object can be a single noun:
    I saw **Colette**.   We visited **Stratford**.

- Objects can also be a string of words based on a noun (a **noun phrase**):
    The children love **a pantomime**.   We won **the match**.

- When you see a string of nouns as a list, think of them as belonging together, all affected by the same action:
    The explosion destroyed **a car, a telephone box, and a shop front**.
  This is not a sequence of three objects, but a single, complex object.

- Pronouns can also be objects, referring to the nouns in other clauses, just as subjects do:
    I found **an egg**. Then I cooked **it**.
  When *I, he, she, we,* and *they* appear as an object, they have a distinct **objective** form.
    Ask **me**.   Ask **him**.   Ask **her**.   Ask **us**.   Ask **them**.
  We do not say:
    *Ask I.   *Ask he.   *Ask she.   *Ask we.   *Ask they.

Activities

A Choose the correct pronoun

In these sentences a non-native speaker, or maybe a young child, has failed to see the difference between subjective and objective forms of the pronouns. Write out the correct versions for Standard English.

1 *You ask they what's happening.
2 *Us are feeling unwell.
3 *Me am reading a book with he.
4 *My uncle has given she a present.
5 *Him has asked we to dinner.

B Find the object

Write out these sentences and underline the object. Look out for sentences with more than one clause, where there may be an object in each.

1 I saw the dentist.
2 Have you met Charlie?
3 The mechanic has fixed it.
4 Jo wants a new pen.
5 I saw the car and bought it.
6 Who's paying the bill?
7 We enjoyed Crete, Cos, and Rhodes.
8 Why don't you invite everyone?
9 I like coffee but Anne likes tea.
10 She's got over 300 books about the Beatles.

C Translate into Alien

Yoda in the 'StarWars' epic has a habit of putting the object in front of the clause, like this:

> **Nine hundred years** have I seen.

Translate the following sentences into Yoda-speak, and underline the objects.

1 I have asked many questions.
2 You are fighting a thousand foes.
3 Evil forces have murdered your father.
4 Your actions will achieve a glorious future for your planet.
5 They have suffered many hardships.
6 You already know the right course of action.
7 I have taught many fine warriors.
8 E.T. has found a telephone.

Clauses with two objects

Sometimes a clause has two objects, as in this sentence:

I / gave / Fred / a sandwich.
S   V   O   O

If we ask, 'What has been given?', the answer is easy: the sandwich. The action of the verb, 'giving', **directly** applies to the sandwich. The sandwich is what has been given. *A sandwich* is therefore called the **direct object** of the verb.

But the action of the verb applies to Fred, too. After all, he is the one who gets the sandwich. He benefits, **indirectly**, from the action of giving. *Fred* is therefore called the **indirect object** of the verb. The indirect object is the person or animal that receives the benefit of an action.

Which way round?

When there are two objects in a clause, you have a choice as to which way round they go.

● You can put the indirect object first:

I gave / Fred / a sandwich.   I bought / Mary / a cake.

Note that it is not possible to say *I gave a sandwich Fred* or *I bought a cake Mary*.

● If you want to put the direct object first, you can do so, but you must add an extra word:

I gave / a sandwich / to Fred.   I bought / a cake / for Mary.

In these kinds of clause, the indirect object usually goes at the end. It doesn't sound quite so natural to say *I gave to Fred a sandwich*. On the other hand, if the direct object starts to become very lengthy, we often do choose this order. Most people prefer to say or write

I gave / to Fred / a beautifully decorated set of stamps from the Republic of South Africa.

rather than

I gave / a beautifully decorated set of stamps from the Republic of South Africa / to Fred.

We like to leave the longest clause element until last.

There are not many verbs which control two objects. Here is a selection of them. Sometimes the direct object comes first and sometimes the indirect object. In each case, you can transform the sentence into the alternative.

I told / my story / to the police.   I'll lend / you / a pound.
We offered / Mary / some help.   Throw / the ball / to your partner.
Will you leave / me / the keys?   Find / a coat / for John.

Activities

A Make the clauses grammatical

There is something odd about the use of the objects in these clauses. Rewrite them so that the sentences feel more acceptable.

1 *I made for the visitors a meal.
2 *The police will find another route the convoy.
3 *I owe a fiver Mary Smith.
4 *Give your answer me.
5 *That short cut will save a great deal of time us.

B Find the two objects

Look at these clauses and work out which is the direct object and which is the indirect object. Draw a line between them, and label the direct object DO and the indirect object IO.

1 We have to pay the garage £100.
2 My kind cousin lent the fare to me.
3 I read a bedtime story to the children.
4 Will you find Mary a pen?
5 The dog brought me my slippers.
6 She offered sweets to her friend.
7 Throw your partner the ball.
8 Have you left a drink for Santa?
9 The teacher told the class the questions.
10 The waitress served some eggs to the customer.

C Change the order: 1

In these sentences, the indirect object always uses the word *to* or *for*. Rewrite them to avoid using these words, like this:

> I gave a cake to Mary. → I gave Mary a cake.

1 They shouldn't deny the prize to Smith.
2 Will you order some chips for me?
3 The home secretary granted a pardon to the two brothers.
4 When you get there, hand the parcel to the gatekeeper.
5 Will you please reserve three seats at the front for me.

D Change the order: 2

In these sentences, the indirect object comes before the direct object. Rewrite them so that the order is the other way round. (Beware: some verbs require *to*; some require *for*.)

1 I promise all the travellers a good time.
2 Can you spare my granny some sugar?
3 They've sent the family another bill.
4 They had to show the audience a different film.
5 We'll try and teach the group another system.

11 *Completing a clause*

The complement element expresses a meaning which adds to that already present in the subject or object. A useful way of remembering its job is to think of the word *complete*: 'the complement completes a meaning'. (Don't mix up its spelling with the word *compliment*, with an *i*, which is a piece of flattery, not a piece of grammar.)

There are two chief kinds of complement.

- The first kind is called a **subject complement**, because it completes the meaning of the subject. It comes after the subject and verb.

  Hilary / is / <u>a doctor</u>.   A tulip / is / <u>a flower</u>.
    S   V   C   S   V   C

  Lucy / was / <u>a lovely baby</u>.
    S   V   C

What comes after the verb identifies very closely with what has gone before the verb. This is what makes a complement different from an object (see p. 42). In *Hilary kicked the ball*, which is **SVO**, there is no identity between *Hilary* and *the ball*. They are totally different things. But in *Hilary is a doctor*, which is **SVC**, the two elements are closely related in meaning.

You can easily feel the 'completing' role of the subject complement if you stop the sentence immediately after the verb: *Hilary is —*, *A tulip is —*. Nothing much has been said until the complement finishes it off.

You can't have a subject complement unless the verb has a special 'linking' meaning. And not many verbs have this function. A form of the verb *be* is the one you will see most often: *is, are, was, were*, etc. Some of the other verbs which have a linking function are shown below. They all have a meaning related to *be*, and you can always replace them by a form of *be*.

  The bull / became / <u>angry</u>.   (In other words, it **was** angry.)
  I / feel / <u>annoyed</u>.   (I **am** annoyed.)
  The weather / is turning / <u>cold</u>.   (It **is** cold.)

- The second kind of complement is called an **object complement**, because it completes the meaning of the direct object. It usually comes immediately after the object. Once again, you can use the verb *be* as a test, to show that there is a link of meaning between the two elements.

  She / made / her friend / <u>angry</u>.   (Her friend **was** angry.)
    S   V   O   C

  They / presumed / the group / <u>lost</u>.   (They **were** lost.)
  I / thought / your children / <u>little angels</u>.   (Your children **were** little angels.)

And, once again, you can try stopping the sentence before the complement, to feel how incomplete it is: *They presumed the group —* , *I thought your children —* .

Activities

A Add a subject complement

Add a subject complement to finish off these incomplete clauses. Check that you've done it correctly by asking yourself whether the subject and the complement both refer to the same thing. Write the clauses out like this:

The kids seem — . → The kids seem restless. → The kids are restless.

1 Elizabeth seems — .
2 The garden looks — at this time of year.
3 Those tyres are becoming — .
4 That drink tastes — in a paper cup.
5 Sue's exam results sound — .
6 Your dog's feeling — .

B Add an object complement

Use one of these words or phrases to make an object complement for these incomplete sentences:

very friendly   easier   a disaster area   hot   wrong

1 The tools have made the job — .
2 I like my coffee — .
3 We've always found the people — in that neighbourhood.
4 They've declared the house — .
5 She'll prove your friend — , you'll see.

C Choose a verb

These clauses all have complements following a form of the verb *be*. Rewrite them with a more interesting verb, using one of these:

spring   remain   fall   turn   sound   smell

1 The music was delightful.
2 They were good friends.
3 The sky was a bright orange and red.
4 The crowd were silent.
5 The cupboard door was open.
6 The coffee is excellent.

D Distinguish the two complements

Write out these sentences, underline the complement, and say whether it belongs to the subject or the object.

1 The door has slammed shut.
2 The wind has slammed the door shut.
3 The weeds are running wild.
4 They're trying to keep the animals quiet.
5 That book will prove very useful for my revision.

Unusual orders

Sometimes, you'll find the order of elements reversed, when people are talking or writing in an emphatic or poetic way. **SVC** becomes **CSV** or **CVS**.

> Very happy / she / was.   Ready and willing / are / we!
>   C   S   V   C   V   S

This is another feature of the way Yoda, the Jedi Master, speaks (see p. 43):

> Strong with the Force / you / are.   Sick / I / 've become.
>   C   S   V   C   S   V

What can be a complement?

- As with subjects and objects, a complement can be a single noun, a string of words based on a noun (a **noun phrase**), or a string of nouns working together as a list.

   > The station's name is <u>Euston</u>.   That man is <u>my uncle</u>.
   > She is <u>a composer and a musician</u>.

   There can never be more than one complement element in a clause.

- Unlike subjects and objects, a complement can be an adjective, a string of words based on an adjective (an **adjective phrase**), or a string of adjectives working together as a list.

   > Mary is <u>cold</u>.   She made me <u>very happy</u>.   We're <u>ready and willing</u>.

   You can't use adjectives as subjects or objects. It is ungrammatical to say such things as *Fierce kicked the ball* or *I saw ready*.

- A complement can also be a pronoun, referring to an earlier noun.

   > That caller was <u>me</u>.   The culprit is <u>him</u>.   The problem is <u>this</u>.

A problem of usage

You'll sometimes find people using the subjective form of the pronoun in such sentences, and saying such things as *It was I* instead of *It was me*. They do this when they are talking or writing very formally and carefully.

This usage was recommended by the first English grammar books, in the 18th century. The authors of these books were influenced by the grammatical patterns they found in Latin, the language of Classical Rome. They thought that Latin was a wonderful language, and believed that English would best develop if it could be shaped to follow the patterns of Latin.

In Latin, the subjective form of a pronoun was **always** used after the verb *to be*. As a result, many generations of schoolchildren were taught to express themselves in English in the same way. But sentences like *It is I* have never been a natural usage in English, and most people find them artificial.

Activities

A Expand the complements

Take these clauses and replace their single-word subject complements with a string of words. Make them as unexpected as possible.

1 I've sprayed the room with disinfectant, and it now smells **lovely**.
2 Wearing those hats, we looked **cool**.
3 Naturally I'm **upset** because we missed the party.
4 My parents have decided to become **students** at the Open University.
5 To suggest that I go to bed at 8 o'clock sounds **sensible**.

B Label the complements

Write out these clauses and underline the complement. Note after each clause whether the complement is (a) a single adjective, (b) an adjective phrase, (c) a noun phrase, (d) a pronoun, or (e) a list of adjectives or nouns.

1 The sea was warm.
2 I can smell them.
3 He was loud and clear.
4 Give me those.
5 She's very pleased.
6 The council elected her the new mayor.
7 The new typist looks keen and clever.
8 That's a lovely gesture.
9 We're absolutely thrilled.
10 I'm both a physicist and an astronomer.

C Decide what follows the verb

In these clauses, forms of the verb *be* are sometimes followed by a complement, and sometimes by some other clause element.

- Mark the clauses which have complements with a C.

- Discuss what is happening in the other clauses. What kind of meaning is being expressed?

1 Mary is an advertising manager.
2 Mary is in London.
3 All of us are terribly busy.
4 I'm not very certain.
5 The band will be there.
6 Be happy.
7 The incident was big news.
8 The meal's on the table.
9 Today is Thursday.
10 The AA man was under the car.

D Write a script

Imagine a conversation between two aliens meeting on Earth for the first time, and describing what they have seen. One alien has been taught to speak by Yoda (as on p. 43), and is using CSV language; the other has not. Write it out as a script, like this:

YODA ALIEN: Full of the Force I am.
OTHER ALIEN: I'm full of the Force, too.

12 *Saying when, where, and how*

There are several ways in which we can put extra meaning into a clause. In particular, we can say when an action took place, where it happened, or how it was performed. The clause element which expresses meanings of this kind is called the **adverbial**.

The adverbial element is very different from the other clause elements.

- One clause can contain several instances:

  Later, / Oscar / kicked / the ball / fiercely / across the field.
  A   S   V   O   A   A

The basic clause pattern is *Oscar kicked the ball* (**SVO**). The three adverbials are 'optional extras': they add new bits of meaning to the sentence, but they don't change the basic meaning. If you left them out, the sentence would still be grammatical.

- Adverbials can be used in several possible positions within the clause – though they most commonly occur at the end. If you take the clause *They asked me*, and want to add the adverbial *often* to it, you will find that it can go in three places:

  Often they asked me.   They often asked me.   They asked me often.

However, we can't say **They asked often me*.

- Adverbials express a wide range of meanings. Here are some of them:

  Time: I left **at 3 o'clock**.   (The adverbial answers the question 'When?')
  Place: I went **to London**.   (The adverbial answers the question 'Where?')
  Manner: I walked **slowly**.   (The adverbial answers the question 'How?')
  Adding a comment: **Frankly**, I think it's right.
  Linking two clauses: The bus was full. **However**, I found a seat.

What can be an adverbial?

- The basic type of adverbial consists of just one word – an adverb. Most adverbs end in *-ly* (see p. 140). A strengthening word like *very* is often used.
  They ran **quickly**.   **Fortunately**, the car wasn't damaged.
  See you **very soon**.

- Another important type is a string of words beginning with a preposition (a **prepositional phrase**):
  They ran **in the garden**.   **After the accident**, the car wasn't damaged.

- Sometimes an adverbial can be just a single noun, or a string of words based on a noun (a **noun phrase**):
  She phoned me **today**.   I went out **this morning**.

Activities

A Add several adverbials

Write out these clauses with some 'optional extra' details, adding adverbial elements to tell us 'when?' or 'where?' or 'how?' Use some of these examples, or make up adverbials of your own.

When?   soon, then, next week, often, today, in the morning, on Sunday
Where?   there, in town, nearby, upstairs, that way, outside, on the table
How?   slowly, loudly, happily, well, like an expert, by car, with haste

1 Our team beat the league champions.
2 I'm doing a new jigsaw.
3 They crossed the park.
4 I saw a huge grasshopper.
5 Joan will speak in the debate.
6 The visitors have arrived.

B Highlight the adverbials

Write out these clauses and highlight anything which is an adverbial.

1 They were speaking quietly.
2 We ran across the road.
3 Slowly, the car turned the corner.
4 Actually, I think she's right.
5 Put it over there on the table.

6 Mike'll be back tomorrow.
7 Have you ever visited France?
8 They then went downstairs.
9 Do you go there often?
10 They gazed sloppily at each other.

C Write a sports commentary

Here is a piece of radio sports commentary. (Punctuation has been added.)

- Rewrite it, taking out all the adverbial elements. Write a brief paragraph explaining how the commentary has changed, and whether you think the new version is better or worse, and why.

Jones scowls angrily at the umpire. He certainly didn't like that call. Still, he's keeping his temper today, and that's the main thing. He serves again now ferociously – into the net. Smith bounces up and down a couple of times, and swipes an imaginary ball into the sky with his racquet. Second service. A better serve that time, makes Smith leap sideways, but he sends a marvellous return across the court, and Jones can't reach it. Smith handled that very coolly and with real power . . .

- Now write another piece of sports commentary, on your favourite sport, putting in as many adverbials as you can think of. Read the results out loud to a group, and decide who would make the best commentator.

13 *Making clause parts agree*

One of the most interesting features of English grammar is the way one clause element can influence another. This especially happens when the subject of a clause changes from singular ('one') to plural ('more than one'). Look at the way the elements change in these clauses.

My friend / is / a pop star.   My friends / are / pop stars.
  S   V   C   S   V   C

If you choose a singular subject, the verb has to be singular and the complement has to be singular. If you choose a plural subject, both other elements change to plural. You cannot say:

    *My friend are pop stars.   *My friends is a pop star.

The elements have to **agree** with each other. They show **agreement**, or **concord**.

There are several other kinds of agreement in English. Note especially:

● The subject must agree with the verb, in the present tense (p. 114). Compare:

    The cat loves milk.   **The cats** love milk.

When the subject is a 'he', 'she' or 'it' (the **third person**: see p. 128), the verb adds an *s*. Note that this happens only with the third person. There is no special ending for *I, we, you,* or *they*:

    I love milk.   You love milk.   We love milk.   They love milk.

There is no special ending to distinguish singular from plural in the past tense. Nor is there a special ending for the 'helping' verbs (see p. 34), such as *can* or *might*.

    The cat loved milk.   The cats loved milk.   She can swim.   They can swim.

The verb *be*

The verb *be* is totally different from all other verbs in the language.

● In the present tense, its third person is an irregular form, *is*.

● It shows agreement after *I*: we have to say *I am*, not **I be, *I is,* or **I are*.

● It is the only verb to show agreement in the past tense, using *was* and *were*.

Here is a list of the *be* forms in Standard English, in the sentence *I — there.*

PRESENT TENSE:	I am there. He / she / it is there.	You / we / they are there.
PAST TENSE:	I / he / she / it was there.	You / we / they were there.

Note that in Standard English we do not say *I were* or *you was* – but you will hear these forms in many local dialects.

Activities

A Show the agreement

Eight of these sentences show agreement between certain clause elements; the other two don't. Write out the eight sentences, and underline the elements which agree with each other.

1 The cat is hungry.
2 We went to town by bus.
3 The doctor's a fine athlete.
4 I was a good runner once.
5 I'm an electronics engineer.
6 The operator will help you.
7 They often talk on the phone.
8 The dogs have gone to sleep.
9 They're looking after themselves.
10 Those two entries are the likely winners.

B Translate into Standard English

These sentences can be heard in some regional dialects, but would be ungrammatical in Standard English. 'Translate' them into Standard English in two ways: (a) by changing the verb, and (b) by changing some other element. Write them out in a table like this:

SENTENCE	CHANGE VERB	CHANGE OTHER ELEMENT
I likes beans.	I like beans.	My cat likes beans.

1 They was ready to go.
2 It were raining a lot last night.
3 I aren't going to help him.
4 Second-hand ones is cheaper.
5 I were only asking about it.
6 I is not interested.

C Analyse the dialect forms

Here are some lines from Mark Twain's *Huckleberry Finn*, written out as a play script. Huck is talking to the slave, Jim. Both are using regional dialect, but you can tell the two people apart.

- Identify the agreement features which distinguish the two speakers.

- Make up some sentences which would be grammatical in Jim's dialect.

- 'Translate' Jim's dialect into Huck's, or Huck's dialect into Jim's. In a group, discuss how this affects the way you 'see' the character.

> HUCK: *But hang it, Jim, you've clean missed the point.*
> JIM: *... I reck'n I knows sense when I sees it ...*
> HUCK: *Looky here, Jim; does a cat talk like we do?*
> JIM: *No, a cat don't.*
> HUCK: *Well, does a cow?*
> JIM: *No, a cow don't ...*

Some problems of usage

People are sometimes uncertain about which agreement rule to use.

- A subject may look singular, but still allow a plural meaning. Which form of the verb *be* would you put in the gap here: *is* or *are*?

     None of the pens — on the table.

None means 'not one', so there are good grounds for expecting the verb to be in the singular: *is*. The speaker might be thinking: 'Not even one is on the table'. However, the speaker is also talking about several pens, and might be thinking 'The pens are not on the table'. So there are good grounds for expecting the verb to be in the plural: *are*. You will find both forms used.

- A subject may look plural, but still allow a singular meaning. Take this one:

     Five years — a long time to be away.

Five years looks plural: it has a plural *-s* ending on the word *year*. So you might expect *are*. But if the speaker is thinking of the 'five years' as a single period of time, you will find *is*.

- When two nouns are linked together as subject, you often have a choice, depending on whether you think of the meanings as one or as separate.

     Law and order — now definitely established in the city.

If you are thinking of *law and order* as a single notion, you will say *is*. If you think of them as two separate notions, *law* and *order*, you will say *are*.

- The same applies to such words as *committee*.

     The committee — meeting again this week.

If you think of committee as a single entity, you will say *is*. If you think of committee as an entity made up of individual units (people), you will say *are*. It's all a matter of point of view. The singular stresses the impersonal unity of the group; the plural the personal identity of its members. Nouns which allow this double perspective are called **collective nouns**.

Which is correct?

People often worry about 'which is correct', in cases like this, and expect grammars to say that one is right and the other is wrong. But everything depends on which meaning is at the front of your mind. You should choose the usage which most closely reflects what you want to say.

Early grammar books did not pay so much attention to the meaning of language, and taught people to follow one usage and avoid the other. This was especially so with *none*, where the grammars would insist on the use of *is* in all circumstances. You'll find that many people prefer to use *none is*, especially in formal writing.

Activities

A Decide on the meaning

In these sentences, the subject could be followed by either a singular verb or a plural verb, depending on how you think of it.

- Choose one of these interpretations, and make up another sentence which illustrates the singular or the plural meaning.

- Underline the words in your sentence which really show the singular or the plural meaning.

Write the examples in a table like this:

SOURCE SENTENCE	INTERPRETATION	YOUR EXAMPLE
The cast was / were brilliant.	Plural	The cast <u>have all</u> gone home to their hotels.
The government is / are behind the times.	Singular	<u>It has</u> got to change <u>its</u> policy.

1 The enemy has / have been defeated.
2 Our gang was / were ready to help.
3 The committee is / are meeting.
4 Your team has / have been playing well.
5 The jury hasn't / haven't reached a verdict.
6 The class is / are being a real pain.
7 The crowd is / are getting angry.
8 A tiny minority is / are against the proposal.
9 My family is / are away this week.
10 The United Nations has / have to decide what to do.

B Explain the meaning of the subject

How is the speaker thinking about the subject, in these sentences? Write a few words by way of interpretation, like this:

EXAMPLE	YOUR INTERPRETATION
Your doctor and guide are downstairs. Six miles is a long way.	The speaker is thinking of two people. The speaker is thinking of six miles as a single distance which has to be travelled.

1 Ten pounds is a lot of money.
2 Bacon and eggs makes a nice meal.
3 My friend and partner is in the other room.
4 England has won the cup.
5 Three quarters of the country was under water.
6 The referee's fairness and impartiality were impressive.

14 *Statements*

What do sentences do? What sorts of meaning do they express? They can argue, persuade, command, ask questions, tell lies, and express hundreds of other notions. But all sentences can be grouped into four basic types: statements, questions, commands, and exclamations. By far the commonest type is the statement.

What is a statement?

A statement is a sentence whose aim is chiefly to convey information. To do this, the clause should contain a subject, and the subject should come in front of the verb.

The children / had / lots of presents.   I / am / hungry.
    <u>S</u>   <u>V</u>   <u>O</u>   <u>S</u> <u>V</u>   <u>C</u>

Most sentences in this book are statements, because the main aim of the book is to provide you with information. Just occasionally, to help make a point more dramatically, you will find a question – such as those at the top of this page – and there are several on the activity pages. You will also find the occasional command, as in the first sentence of the paragraph below. But textbooks, like newspapers, are giving you information, so they rarely contain sentences other than statements.

Any exceptions?

- Look out for cases in conversation where the subject is left out:

  Told you so.   Looks like rain.

  These are still statements, because we know that they are short for *I told you so* and *It looks like rain.*

This kind of usage is common only when you are speaking casually, and it is obvious what the subject-matter is. You will never hear it in formal speech, nor see it in writing – unless, of course, you are trying to write down exactly how people talk, such as in a novel. If you leave out the subject, your sentence may not make sense, or be ambiguous, as here:

  Jim and Mike met Jane at the club. Asked her to marry him.
Who's hoping to marry Jane?

- Also look out for a rather unusual kind of sentence, where the subject **follows** the verb, but the sentence is still a statement. If you begin a sentence with the word *scarcely*, you have to change the word order in this way:

  Scarcely had she left the room when the phone rang.
  It isn't grammatical to say:

  *Scarcely she had left the room when the phone rang.

There are very few words which cause the word order to change like this. *Barely* and *hardly* are two more. They are all words with a strongly negative meaning.

Activities

A Decide which are statements

Which of the following sentences give you information, and which do not? You will need to think carefully about the meaning, as there are no punctuation marks to help you.

- Put full-stops after the sentences which are statements.

- Put question marks or exclamation marks after the other sentences.

1 Oil floats on water
2 What time is it
3 I've bought a new CD
4 Sit down
5 Where's the sugar
6 Henry VIII had six wives
7 The books weren't on the shelf
8 Give me a break
9 Can you see me at 3 o'clock
10 I'm not feeling very well

B Find the informal statements

Some of these sentences can easily survive without their subject, in casual conversation. Decide which they are, and write them out in a casual speech style.

1 I beg your pardon.
2 A dog was chasing a cat.
3 I told you it would rain.
4 I don't know what to say.
5 The operator told me the number.
6 It looks like there'll be snow.
7 My friend knows what to say.
8 It sounds fine to me.
9 The manager served me a drink.
10 It serves you right.

C Analyse what a statement does

Statements can give information about all kinds of things – such as facts, beliefs, and opinions. Some report the truth; some exaggerate; some tell lies. Write a sentence after each of the following statements to say what kind of information it is giving you, in the following way:

> Oil floats on water.   This statement expresses a scientific fact.
> I hate getting up early.   This statement expresses a personal feeling.

1 Our TV is broken.
2 I think it's going to rain.
3 A cactus is a kind of desert plant.
4 I like onions.
5 John is a splendid fellow.
6 The Battle of Trafalgar was in 1805.
7 I love lots of homework.
8 A computer is an intelligent being.
9 God is love.
10 I really must thank you for your letter.

D Write about a topic

Write five statements about one of the following topics. Make them of different kinds, as in C.

> fog   cheese   dinosaurs   dentists

15 *Questions*

Questions are sentences which ask for information. In writing, we show that a sentence is a question by ending it with a question mark (?). In speech, we can use a questioning tone of voice.

Questions fall into three main types, depending on the kind of reply they expect, and on how they are constructed.

● Some questions allow a reply which can be simply *yes* or *no*. The subject follows the first verb. These are called **yes-no questions**.

    Are / the tickets / ready?   Did / you / get / my letter?
     <u>V</u>   <u>S</u>   <u>C</u>   <u>V</u>   <u>S</u>   <u>O</u>

Here the answers can be simply *yes* or *no* – or of course *don't know*!

● Some questions allow a reply from a wide range of possibilities. These begin with a question word, such as *what*, *why*, *where*, *when*, or *how*. They are called **wh-questions** (pronounced 'double-u aitch').

    Where was the car going?   Why didn't they answer?

Here you can't answer with *yes* or *no* – you have to provide some extra information.

    Where was the car going?   *No.
    Where was the car going?   To the garage.

● Some questions require a reply which relates to the choices given in the sentence. The questions always contain the connecting word *or*. They are called **alternative questions**.

    Will you travel by train or by boat?

Here you are being given a choice of just two answers: *by train* or *by boat*. Of course, you can always reject the alternatives and opt for something else: *neither*!

Tone of voice?

A simple way of turning a statement into a yes-no question is just to add a questioning tone of voice. These sentences look like statements, but they function as if they were questions. To show this effect in writing, you put a question mark after the statement. Compare these two sentences:
    You've spoken to her.   (A statement. 'I'm telling you.')
    You've spoken to her?   A question. 'I'm asking you.')
This speech pattern has become very popular in recent years, especially among young people.

Activities

A Separate the question types

Decide whether these sentences are yes-no questions (Y/N), wh-questions (WH), alternative questions (A), or tone-of-voice questions (TV). Write an answer to each.

1 Where's the salt?
2 Are they staying for dinner?
3 How did they escape?
4 Is it sunny or raining?
5 Have you ever been to Disneyland?
6 They're arriving on Monday?
7 What time is it?
8 Were they in Paris or Rome?
9 Who's there?
10 You're not joking?

B Decide about difficulty

Here are three questions about the same subject-matter.

YES-NO QUESTION:	Did World War 2 end in 1945?
ALTERNATIVE QUESTION:	Did World War 2 end in 1944 or 1945?
WH-QUESTION:	When did World War 2 end?

- In a group, discuss which of these questions is (a) the easiest to answer, and (b) the hardest to answer.

- Teachers spend a lot of their time asking questions. Carry out a small survey to see which type of question they use most. Do types of question differ between English, maths, history, and other subjects?

C Discuss asking and telling

In this extract from Charles Dickens's *Great Expectations* (Chapter 19), Miss Havisham interrogates Pip using tone-of-voice questions.

'So you go tomorrow?'
'Yes, Miss Havisham.'
'And you are adopted by a rich person?'
'Yes, Miss Havisham.'
'Not named?'
'No, Miss Havisham.'
'And Mr. Jaggers is made your guardian?'
'Yes, Miss Havisham.'

- In a group, discuss what the use of this type of question suggests about the speaker? Imagine the tone of voice in which she might say them. Is she asking or telling?

- Write out the dialogue again, but change Miss Havisham's sentences into yes-no questions (e.g. 'So are you going tomorrow?'). How does this alter the tone of the conversation?

Not replying

Most questions expect a reply. It isn't sociable to ignore a question, and say nothing. People would think you were rude – or perhaps ill. But there are two kinds of question which require no reply at all.

- Some sentences look like questions in their structure, but are more like exclamations. These sentences are used to express a strong feeling, where you're asking your listener to agree. Imagine you are getting a visit from relatives who have not seen you for a long time. The visitors will very likely say:

    Haven't you grown?

This is not really a question. They're not asking you for information, as they would if they asked *Haven't you got a dog now?* The visitors are telling you: 'You have grown'. In writing, it usually appears with an exclamation mark: *Haven't you grown!*

On the other hand, you can, if you want, respond to such a sentence, and say *Yes*, or make some other embarrassed remark. Parents often reply on their child's behalf. So there is still a hint of a questioning element in such sentences. They are therefore called **exclamatory questions**.

- Another type of question which doesn't require a reply is called a **rhetorical question**. You do not expect an answer. If you say:

    Can I help it if he's an idiot?

you would be somewhat surprised to hear someone say, *Yes, you can.* Other common rhetorical questions are *Who cares?* and *How should I know?* And in political speeches you will often hear some quite complex rhetorical questions:

    Why do we have to put up with this state of affairs any longer?

Tags

A common type of yes-no question keeps the word order the same as in a statement, and leaves the questioning bit until the end.

    It's in the hall, **isn't it**?   She's not in, **is she**?

These are called **tag questions**, because they are 'tagged on' at the end of the sentence. In casual conversation, you often find these questions replaced by a single word, such as *right?* or *OK?* Tags are not usually found in writing, unless you are representing a conversation.

Note that the meaning of a tag question in speech depends on how you say it. If you alter the tune of the voice, you can change the meaning. When the pitch rises, the sentence is 'asking'. When the pitch falls, the sentence is 'telling'. In writing, punctuation shows the difference:

    She's not in, is she?   (rising = asking = 'I really want to know')
    She's not in, is she!   (falling = telling = 'I told you so!')
Sometimes people are forced to say 'Are you asking me or telling me?'

Activities

A Distinguish the question types

- Decide whether the following sentences are likely to be rhetorical questions (R), exclamatory questions (E), or questions which genuinely require an answer (Q). Add a question mark or an exclamation mark, as appropriate.

1 What can I say to you	6 Where's Uncle Fred going
2 Am I hungry	7 Can I help it if they're late
3 Is there some cheese in the fridge	8 What difference does it make
4 Wasn't it a splendid concert	9 Ten A grades. Hasn't she done well
5 Where's the world going	10 Who's got money these days

- Practise saying the sentences aloud in an appropriate tone of voice.

B Choose a meaning

- Choose an 'asking' or a 'telling' interpretation for each of the following sentences, and add a question mark (for asking) or an exclamation mark (for telling). Then write a follow-up sentence in support. Here are two examples:

> The car was new, wasn't it → The car was new, wasn't it! I remember Jim telling me it was.
> She isn't outside, is she → She isn't outside, is she? I've been looking for her all morning.

1 Ann didn't speak to you, did she
2 You're Michael Smith, aren't you
3 Your gloves aren't in the kitchen, are they
4 The butler did the murder, didn't he
5 I'll be able to get a new job, won't I

- Practise saying these sentences aloud, in an appropriate 'asking' or 'telling' tone of voice.

C Write a question sketch

Write a brief sketch for two characters who speak only in questions. Try to vary the type of questions they use. Here's an example of how a sketch might start:

[At the travel agent's]
A: Can I book a ticket to Florida?
B: Do you want to go by air or boat?
A: Which do you advise?
B: How much do you want to pay?
A: Do I look rich?
B: Isn't that a very expensive watch on your wrist?
A: Is that any of your business? . . .

16 *Commands*

There are many ways in which you can tell someone to do something. Here are some of them.

- Instructing   Sit down immediately!

- Inviting   Come over to watch a video tonight.

- Warning   Mind your head.

- Pleading   Help me!

- Advising   Take an aspirin.

- Requesting   Open the window, please.

- Expressing good wishes   Have a nice day!

These sentences are all constructed in the same way. In each case, the verb is in its basic form, with no endings, and there is no subject element present. Sentences of this kind are called **commands**. Many commands consist of just a verb:

> Stop!   Jump!   Help!   Go!   Fetch!

Some variations

There are just a few ways in which you can vary this sentence pattern.

- For extra emphasis, you can add a subject:

    <u>You</u> be quiet!   <u>Everyone</u> move!   <u>All you children</u> sit down!

- When you are talking to other people, you can begin the sentence with *do*, *don't*, or *do not*.

    <u>Do</u> come in.   <u>Don't</u> do that.   <u>Do not</u> cross the road.

- When you are talking to yourself, or to the group of which you are a member, you can begin the sentence with *let*, followed by a subject. In casual speech, *let us* is usually shortened to *let's*.

    <u>Let</u> me see.   <u>Let</u> us pray.   <u>Let's</u> go.

Note that this use of *let* is very different from the verb *let* meaning 'permit'. *Let us go* meaning 'shall we go?' is not the same as *Let us go* meaning 'free us'. Only the first can be shortened to *Let's go*. It makes sense for prisoners to say to their captors *Let us go*: they want to leave their captors behind. It wouldn't make sense for them to say *Let's go*: that would be to invite their captors to go with them!

Activities

A Decide on different uses

- Look at each of these commands, and decide what sort of use they have, using the headings on the facing page (instructing, inviting, etc.).

1 Give me a break!   4 Look out!   7 Please lend me your book.
2 Let's party!   5 Get out!   8 Enjoy your meal.
3 Be careful!   6 Meet me outside Smith's.   9 Keep your money safe.

- Can you think of any other uses which commands might have?

B Find the commands

Here is an extract from one of Joyce Grenfell's comedy sketches about a teacher in a nursery school: 'Story time'. See how many commands you can find. Look out for those which begin with *do* or *let* or which have the subject expressed.

> *Children ... pay attention, please. Free time is over, so put away your things and*
> *we are going to tell our nice story, so come over here and make a circle on the floor*
> *all around me, and we'll tell the story together. We've got a visitor today, so we can*
> *tell the story to her. ...*
> *Hurry up everybody. Don't push – there's lots of room for us all. ...*
> *Edgar, let go of Timmy's ear and settle down.*
> *Come along, everybody.*
> *Sidney, come out from under the table and join in the fun.*
> *No, you're not a space rocket.*
> *You can't wait for the count-down, you come out now. ...*
> *And stop machine-gunning everybody, please. ...*
> *Let's have some nice straight backs, shall we?*

What impression of the situation does this language give you? Do all teachers talk like this?

C Alter the force

Commands can sound very abrupt. Choose a command, and think of ways in which you can alter its force, making it sound more polite or friendly. At what point do you have to change the type of sentence, and start making use of statements and questions? Here are some examples, starting with the command *Pass the salt.*

> Pass the salt, please.
> Would you be so kind as to pass the salt?
> I'd really be most awfully pleased if you would pass me the salt.

Try putting the examples on a scale, running from **most formal** to **most informal**. In a group, discuss the occasions when you might really use these examples.

17 Exclamations

An exclamation is a sentence which shows that a person's feelings have been suddenly aroused. The speaker (or writer) has been shocked, impressed, surprised, disgusted, delighted – indeed, affected by any emotion, as long as it is felt strongly. In writing, there is a special punctuation mark designed to show that a sentence is uttered with extra feeling: the **exclamation mark** (!).

Any type of sentence can be uttered in a strong tone of voice, and if you wanted to show this in writing, you would use an exclamation mark. This statement, question, and command are all doing their usual jobs, but are being uttered with extra force:

> STATEMENT: You played that brilliantly!
> QUESTION: Were you in the town centre on the night of 12 August?!
> COMMAND: Sit down now!

However, there are some kinds of sentence whose **only** job is to be an exclamation. The commonest take the form of a single word or short phrase. Some are little more than noises – but they still have a clear emotional meaning.

> Gosh! Oh dear! Yuk! Phew! Of all the cheek!

Other kinds of exclamation have a full clause structure, as these examples show:

- In their fullest form, the first element in the clause begins with the word *what* or *how*, and this is followed by the subject and the verb, in that order.

> <u>What a lovely day</u> it is! <u>How nice</u> they look!

There is also a shorter form, which uses only the first element: *What a lovely day! How nice!*

Very rarely, you'll find a *how* or *what* followed by a verb and a subject, in that order.

> <u>How often</u> have I cursed that terrible day!
> <u>What a fine picture</u> does Shakespeare present in this play!

You might find these when people are making a formal speech, or writing in a literary style.

More than one exclamation mark?

If the emotion is very strong, people use several exclamation marks – but only in very informal writing: *And they've invited me to go with them!!!!!* On the other hand, in serious writing, such as textbooks, there are usually no exclamation marks at all. There is no need for them, as authors usually present their subject unemotionally. Similarly, exclamation marks are not very appropriate in a school essay, unless there is a good reason for expressing your feelings.

Activities

A What emotional meaning is expressed by these exclamatory noises?

1 Boo!	4 Pooh!	7 Oops!	10 Grrr!
2 Oho!	5 Wow!	8 Yippee!	11 Hmm!
3 Ouch!	6 Gosh!	9 Aha!	12 Alas!

B Turn statements into exclamations

Turn these statements into exclamations with a full clause structure, beginning with *what* or *how*. Then reduce the exclamation to a short form. Write them out like this:

It's a lovely day. → What a lovely day it is! → What a lovely day!

1 It was a marvellous show.	6 That house looks weird.
2 We're in an awful mess.	7 This is a very noisy party.
3 They were stupid.	8 A huge crowd is in the street.
4 We've been waiting a long time.	9 That story is unbelievable.
5 The wind is awful.	10 They had very bad luck.

C Remove the exclamation marks

Here are some exclamatory sentences. Write them out without the exclamation mark, then add a comment saying what the difference in meaning could be.

1 Charming!	4 He was wearing a purple (!) hat.
2 No more noise!	5 The light's red!!
3 This is a one-way street!	6 Another brilliant essay, I see, Smith!

D Judge the effect

This passage from Jane Austen's *Pride and Prejudice* (Chapter 40) is spoken by the eldest Bennet daughter, Jane, with great feeling. Any of the sentences might have ended in an exclamation mark, but only certain sentences are given one.

- In a group, discuss how the exclamation marks influence the way you would read the passage aloud. Rewrite the passage putting them in different places, and compare the result.

- What would be the effect of (a) leaving them all out, or (b) putting one after every sentence?

'I do not know when I have been more shocked,' said she. 'Wickham so very bad! It is almost past belief. And poor Mr. Darcy! dear Lizzy, only consider what he must have suffered. Such a disappointment! and with the knowledge of your ill opinion too! and having to relate such a thing of his sister! It is really too distressing. I am sure you must feel it so.'

Nouns and Noun Phrases

3 Nouns and noun phrases

A noun phrase is the main construction which can appear as the subject, object, or complement of a clause. In its simplest form, it consists of just a **noun**.

<u>Ostriches</u> can't fly.   I like **buns**.   These are **sentences**.

But more often the noun is the centre, or **head**, of a string of words, as in the examples below. These noun-based strings are called **noun phrases**.

Buns	taste nice.
The **buns**	taste nice.
All the **buns**	taste nice.
All the currant **buns**	taste nice.
All the currant **buns** in the window	taste nice.

Despite all the other words in the phrase, each of these sentences is about the same thing: *buns*.

Part 3 is all about noun phrases. They appear in various shapes and sizes. Many are very short, consisting of just two or three words. But some noun phrases consist of dozens of words. Disentangling the structure of a long and complex noun phrase can be quite tricky. Fortunately, as we shall see, all noun phrases have the same basic structure.

We begin with nouns, the most important part of the noun phrase.

18 *Nouns*

The noun is one of the chief types of word in English grammar. Most major sentences contain at least one noun; and most of the words in a dictionary are nouns. Nouns are obviously very useful.

Nouns are useful because they carry out a 'naming' function. The term actually comes from a Latin word, *nomen*, which meant 'name'. One of the earliest language-using activities in children, around the age of 1, is to start naming things.

So what can be named? Far more than just things (*chair, pen*). Nouns also name people (*Joan, Mr Smith*), animals (*duck, anaconda*), places (*London, France*), and a wide range of processes and concepts (*advice, beauty, addition*).

The grammar of the noun

How can we recognize that a word is a noun? There are several grammatical clues in a sentence. It isn't even necessary to know what the words mean. If I borrow some nonsense from Lewis Carroll, and call you *a slithy tove*, you know that *tove* is a noun, even though you may not be sure what it is. How do you know?

A word is a noun if some of these factors apply:

- It comes directly under the influence of a word like *a* or *the* : *a car, the cat* (see p. 88).

- It acts as the most important word in a noun phrase, as in *the big* <u>*house*</u> *on the hill*.

- It can add a suffix (see p. 12) to express singular and plural, as in *dog* / *dogs*.

- It can add a suffix to express such meanings as possession, as in *children's toys*.

Look at the ending

You can often tell that a word is a noun by looking at the way it has been built up. Many words become nouns by adding a special noun-forming suffix to another word. For example, if you begin with the adjective *kind* (as in *a kind person*), you can add *-ness* to make the noun *kindness*. If you begin with the verb *refer*, you can add *-ee* and make *referee*. Here are some others (beware the occasional spelling change):

> exploit + -ation → exploitation   ideal + -ism → idealism
> rapid + -ity → rapidity   amaze + -ment → amazement
> profit + -eer → profiteer   survive + -or → survivor

Some suffixes can even form one kind of noun out of another kind of noun. *Book* is a noun, but if you add *-let*, you get *booklet* – another noun. Here are some others:

> king + -dom → kingdom   spoon + -ful → spoonful
> boy + -hood → boyhood   friend + -ship → friendship
> slave + -ery → slavery   gang + -ster → gangster

Activities

A Decide what is named

Here is a long list of nouns. Decide what is being named, in each case – such as (a) a thing, (b) a person, (c) a place, (d) a time, (e) a concept, or (f) an activity.

1 Paris	6 museum	11 irritation	16 geography
2 month	7 teapot	12 morning	17 money
3 grandmother	8 Lisa	13 nightmare	18 fright
4 caravan	9 accident	14 idea	19 pocket
5 trouble	10 Tuesday	15 biography	20 quietness

B Find the noun

Each of these sentences contains an example of a noun. Find the noun, and in each case say which 'clue(s)' helped you. The first one is done for you.

EXAMPLE	NOUN	CLUE?
the carpet was blue	carpet	because it has *the* directly before it

1 I've found a wallet.
2 Who's seen my new pen?
3 Cows aren't scary.
4 There was happiness everywhere.
5 I've been to Mary's.
6 I just want the bare necessities.
7 The problem is sure to go away.
8 I can see stars.
9 He looked at me with amazement.
10 The hens have got out.

C Use the suffix

Here is a list of nouns formed by adding a suffix. Identify the suffix, and use a dictionary to find three more words which use the same suffix.

1 consultation	2 handful	3 ringlet	4 solidity	5 loyalist
6 writer	7 princess	8 socialite	9 contestant	10 profiteer

D Survey nouns in titles

Here are the titles of some famous novels. Underline the words which are nouns. Include any nouns which are being used before other nouns, in an adjective-like way (as in A *Christmas* Carol).

1 Pride and Prejudice	2 Tender is the Night	3 The Mayor of Casterbridge	4 Cider with Rosie
5 July's People	6 Animal Farm	7 The Great Gatsby	8 Jane Eyre

- There are 23 words in these 8 titles. Count the nouns, and work out how likely it is that a word in a title will be a noun. Check your result against a sample of titles in the school library.

- In a group, discuss why nouns should be so important in book-titles.

19 *Different kinds of noun*

Nouns can be grouped into six main types. The first division is into **proper** and **common** nouns. Common nouns can then be divided into **count** and **noncount** types. And both of these can be further divided into **concrete** and **abstract** types.

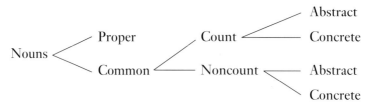

Common and proper nouns

As the name suggests, most nouns are common nouns. A common noun refers to a whole class of things: when you say *An aardvark eats ants*, the word *aardvark* doesn't refer to just one particular animal but to all possible aardvarks.

On the other hand, if you had an aardvark called *Fred*, *Fred* would be a proper noun, because you are now thinking of a particular aardvark. A proper noun is a word which names a specific person, animal, place, time, occasion, and so on:

> Mary   Liverpool   Tuesday   Snowdon   Christmas

Most proper nouns do not appear in a dictionary.

You can often have a series of proper nouns working together. Your name, for example, consists of at least two nouns: a first name and a surname. Here are some other examples: *Queen Elizabeth*, *Easter Sunday*, *Silas Marner*, *Sherlock Holmes*.

Sometimes a word can be either a common noun or a proper noun, depending on how you use it. Compare the sentence *There are several moons around that planet* with *I looked up at the moon*. When *moon* means 'earth satellite', it refers to a single, specific thing. It is a proper noun – and is often written with a capital letter, *Moon*.

Capital letters?

A proper noun usually begins in writing with a capital letter – as in most of the examples on this page. But we have seen that *moon* may or may not have a capital letter, and the same applies to several other words, such as *the bible* or *the Bible*, *the earth* or *the Earth*, *god* or *God*. You will find both spellings used.

Not all words beginning with a capital letter are nouns, as you can see in many book titles, such as *The Great Gatsby*. The pronoun *I* is always spelled with a capital. Also, capitals can be used in humorous writing for a mock epic effect:

> It was going to be The Concert Of The Century.

Activities

A Distinguish proper from common

Here is a list of common and proper nouns – but all capital letters are missing. See if you can tell from the sense which are the proper nouns, and write them out with an initial capital letter.

1 james	6 wednesday	11 america
2 bottle	7 architect	12 rainbow
3 birmingham	8 carrot	13 easter
4 beetles	9 spain	14 everest
5 beatles	10 ghost	15 summer

B Use nouns in two ways

These nouns could be either proper or common. Think up two sentences which show that they are different in meaning. Give the proper noun an initial capital letter, like this:

sun	COMMON NOUN USE:	There are millions of suns in the universe.
	PROPER NOUN USE:	Don't look at the Sun through a telescope.

1 queen	6 party	
2 channel	7 bishop	
3 war	8 revolution	
4 bishop	9 south	
5 continent	10 cabinet	

C Discuss different effects

Here are two verses from Oscar Wilde's *The Ballad of Reading Gaol*. Find examples of the different ways in which capital letters are used: (a) to show a proper noun, (b) to show the name of something, (c) to show a special use of a common noun, (d) to give a phrase an 'epic' status, and (e) to help show that the language is poetry.

> *The Governor was strong upon*
> *The Regulations Act:*
> *The Doctor said that Death was but*
> *A scientific fact;*
> *And twice a day the Chaplain called,*
> *And left a little tract.*

> *With slouch and swing around the ring*
> *We trod the Fools' Parade!*
> *We did not care: we knew we were*
> *The Devil's Own Brigade:*
> *And shaven head and feet of lead*
> *Make a merry masquerade.*

Carry out a similar activity using some other texts, such as a chapter of a novel or a section from a school textbook. Do you find any differences in the way proper nouns are used? Would you expect to find more proper nouns in a short story, a history book, or a science book? Why?

Count and noncount nouns

Common nouns can be divided into two types. **Count** (or **countable**) nouns refer to individual units you can count, such as *books*, *eggs*, and *horses*. **Noncount** (or **mass**) nouns refer to things or concepts which cannot be thought of as a collection of separate units, such as *butter*, *music*, and *advice*.

You can always tell the difference between a count and a noncount use of a noun by the grammar.

- Count nouns cannot stand alone in the singular, whereas noncount nouns can.

    *Book is red.   Music is fun.

So, *book* is a count noun, and *music* is a noncount noun.

- Count nouns allow a plural, whereas noncount nouns do not.

    books   eggs   *musics   *advices

- Count nouns occur in the singular with the word *a*, whereas noncount nouns take *some*. (Both types can occur with *the*.)

    I'd like a book.   *I'd like a music.   *I'd like an advice.
    *I'd like some book.   I'd like some music.   I'd like some advice.
    I like the book.   I like the music.   I like the advice.

Some nouns can be either count or noncount, depending on their meaning. Compare these sentences:

    Have you bought a paper?   Have you bought paper?

The first use is countable: it is a newspaper. The second use is uncountable: it is paper in general.

Abstract and concrete nouns

Both count and noncount nouns can be divided further into abstract and concrete types.

- Concrete nouns refer to things whose dimensions can be plotted and measured, such as *book*, *referee*, *dog*, *butter*, and *windmill*.

- Abstract nouns refer to general ideas or qualities, such as *kindness*, *difficulty*, *condition*, *speed* and *truth*.

It is often quite difficult to decide just how concrete or abstract a word is. Many nouns can be interpreted in either an abstract or a concrete way, depending on how they are being used. *Music*, for example, is concrete when you think of it as represented in a score, but it is abstract when you think of it as does Duke Orsino in *Twelfth Night*: 'If music be the food of love . . .'. *Life* is a fairly abstract notion in *Isn't life wonderful*, but it becomes very concrete when it is weighed against cash in *Your money or your life!*

Activities

A Distinguish count and noncount

This list contains count and noncount nouns. Decide which is which, and check your decision by seeing whether the noun can (a) stand alone, (b) take a plural, or (c) occur with *a*. Write them out like this.

computer	COUNT	You can't say *Computer is expensive.*
		You can say *computers.*
		You can say *a computer.*

1 wall	6 diary	11 farm
2 courage	7 violence	12 traffic
3 sunshine	8 pig	13 photography
4 shoulder	9 harm	14 princess
5 chess	10 leisure	15 dictionary

B Look at the context

These nouns could be either count or noncount, depending on the context. Write out two sentences which would show the difference.

1 television	2 light	3 lamb	4 experience	5 beauty
6 cheese	7 drink	8 decoration	9 diet	10 mint

C Analyse a style

Examine this passage from George Orwell's *Animal Farm* (Chapter 9) and list the nouns as **abstract**, **concrete**, or **unclear** in three columns. Write a sentence commenting on any cases you cannot decide.

> At the *beginning*, when the *laws* of Animal Farm were first formulated, the retiring *age* had been fixed for *horses* and *pigs* at twelve, for *cows* at fourteen, for *dogs* at nine, for *sheep* at seven, and for *hens* and *geese* at five. Liberal old age *pensions* had been agreed upon. As yet no *animal* had actually retired on *pension*, but of late the *subject* had been discussed more and more. Now that the small *field* beyond the *orchard* had been set aside for *barley*, it was rumoured that a *corner* of the large *pasture* was to be fenced off and turned into a *grazing-ground* for superannuated *animals*. For a *horse*, it was said, the *pension* would be five *pounds* of *corn* a *day* and, in *winter*, fifteen *pounds* of *hay*, with a *carrot* or possibly an *apple* on public *holidays*. Boxer's twelfth *birthday* was due in the late *summer* of the following *year*.

On the whole, would you say this was a 'concrete' or an 'abstract' style? Compare it with a paragraph taken from a textbook. Are there any differences?

20 *Singular and plural*

Most nouns have both a singular and a plural form, expressing the difference between 'one' and 'more than one'. The vast majority change from singular to plural in a completely predictable way, by adding an *-s* ending. This is the **regular** plural form, as seen in thousands of nouns:

> cats   flutes   pterodactyls   dictionaries   potatoes   boxes

Look out for the words where the spelling at the end of the noun has to change.

Irregular nouns

There are only a few dozen nouns with an **irregular** plural form. Very young children often get them wrong, as do foreigners with a poor command of English. You might hear a 4–year–old say *mouses* instead of *mice*, or a new adult learner say *knifes* instead of *knives*. Because these are the awkward cases, grammar books always concentrate on them. But don't forget that they are a tiny group, compared with the regular nouns.

- Some nouns do not change at all, as they go from singular to plural. If someone says *I like your sheep*, you do not know if it is one sheep or several. Here are some others with a 'zero' plural.

  > deer   cod   Swiss   Japanese   p (= pence)
  > aircraft   offspring   dice

- Seven nouns form a plural by changing their vowel:

  > man → men   foot → feet   goose → geese   mouse → mice
  > woman → women   tooth → teeth   louse → lice

If the noun has a special sense, it stays regular. In Disneyland, we talk about people dressed up as *Mickey Mouses*, not as **Mickey Mice*!

- Four nouns add *-en*, in two cases changing the vowel as well:

  > ox → oxen   child → children   brother → brethren
  > aurochs → aurochsen

- A few nouns change their final *-f* to *-v* and then add *-s*:

  > knife → knives   wife → wives   loaf → loaves   half → halves

People are often uncertain about how to use several of the nouns in this group. Should we say *hoofs* or *hooves*? *scarfs* or *scarves*? *dwarfs* or *dwarves*? This is one of the areas where the language is changing, so you must expect to find people differing in their choice of these alternatives. The irregular forms are slowly being replaced by regular ones. In the title of the film, Snow White meets seven *dwarfs*.

Activities

A Distinguish regular from irregular

Examine this list of noun plurals and decide which are regular (R) and which are irregular (I).

1 calves	6 streets	11 children	16 examples
2 monkeys	7 leaves	12 hands	17 mice
3 women	8 photographs	13 feet	18 vets
4 rulers	9 salmon	14 wolves	19 elves
5 spacecraft	10 buttons	15 dinners	20 bison

B Correct the errors

A foreign learner has made a plural error in each of the following sentences. Make the appropriate corrections.

1 *I have just made some new shelfs.
2 *The dog is chasing the sheeps.
3 *Two oxes pulled the plough.
4 *The thiefs were very daring.
5 *Many Germen were in Crete.
6 *Several people lost their lifes.
7 *The hunters shot three deers.
8 *Postmans get up very early.
9 *I saw some mongeese at the zoo.
10 *The Portugueses were good explorers.

C Use both forms

You cannot tell whether the following nouns are singular or plural until you use them in a sentence with a singular or plural verb. Both are possible. Write out two sentences for each example which show the two meanings. The first one is done for you.

spacecraft   SINGULAR: The spacecraft was in danger of crashing.
PLURAL: Modern spacecraft are very expensive.

1 hovercraft	6 species
2 crossroads	7 steelworks
3 gallows	8 series
4 kennels	9 oats
5 offspring	10 barracks

D Turn into Standard English

In some dialects, people often use a singular noun of measurement with a plural meaning. Here are some examples. Turn them into Standard English.

1 I reckon the gap is 50 foot.
2 She bought it for five pound.
3 He must weigh 20 stone at least.
4 They delivered three ton of coal.
5 We saw them about five mile back.

Nouns of foreign origin

Nouns which have been borrowed from foreign languages pose a problem.

- Some of these nouns have taken on the regular native plural inflection:

    chorus → choruses   circus → circuses

- Some have kept the plural inflection from the original language:

    oasis → oases   bacterium → bacteria

- And some allow both native and foreign inflections:

    cactus → cactuses **and** cacti   formula → formulas **and** formulae

In these cases, the regular form tends to be the one used in everyday conversation. The irregular form is more likely when you are thinking of the subject in a technical way. Botanists tend to talk about *cacti*, and scientists about *formulae*.

Unfortunately, there are no rules. You have to learn the plural along with the noun when you meet it for the first time. Then keep your ears open for changes in usage.

Some foreign plurals

Source / ending	Foreign plural	Native plural	Both plurals
Latin -us	stimulus → stimuli	virus → viruses	fungus → funguses, fungi
Latin -a	larva → larvae	drama → dramas	antenna → antennae, antennas
Latin -um	erratum → errata	museum → museums	aquarium → aquaria, aquariums
Greek -on	criterion → criteria	electron → electrons	automaton → automata, automatons
French -eau	gateau → gateaux	Cointreau → Cointreaus	bureau → bureaux, bureaus
Italian -o	graffito → graffiti	soprano → sopranos	virtuoso → virtuosi, virtuosos

Note that, sometimes, the different plurals express different meanings. The plural of *appendix* is *appendixes* or *appendices*. But you will find *appendices* inside books, and *appendixes* inside bodies. Similarly, tiny raised numerals in maths are *indices*, not *indexes*; and little darlings at play may be *cherubs*, but they are not *cherubim*.

Don't exaggerate the difficulty of foreign plurals. There are not many of them. There are hundreds of words in English ending in *-on*, for example, but only a small number come from Greek, and only some allow a plural in *-a*. Words like the following add *-s*, like any normal noun.

    carbon   electron   horizon   lion   marathon   pylon   skeleton

Similarly, we have *cameras*, not **camerae*, and *minibuses*, not **minibi*.

Activities

A Decide on the plural

Here is a list of foreign-looking nouns, but only some of them allow an irregular plural. Write the correct plural in each case. Use a dictionary, if you need to.

1 geranium	6 alga	11 pendulum	16 phylum
2 phenomenon	7 crocus	12 tympano	17 genus
3 foetus	8 memorandum	13 prospectus	18 papyrus
4 millennium	9 encyclopedia	14 spectrum	19 crisis
5 commando	10 brontosaurus	15 studio	20 maximum

B Make some corrections

A non-native speaker of English has added an *-s* or *-es* to these nouns. Some are right; some are wrong. Make corrections, then use the plural in a sentence.

LEARNER'S FORM	CORRECTION	USE IN SENTENCE
phenomenons	phenomena	We saw some marvellous phenomena through the telescope.
medallions	not needed	The dictator wore three large medallions.

1 graffitos	6 curriculums	11 metropolises	16 dilemmas
2 censuses	7 stimuluses	12 tympanos	17 opinions
3 criterions	8 aquariums	13 premiums	18 diagnosises
4 millenniums	9 portfolios	14 liaisons	19 bonuses
5 phobias	10 gateaus	15 crisises	20 larvas

C Choose the right plural

These nouns have two plurals, but the usage is different. Choose the form which is appropriate for each sentence; then explain why. The first one is done for you.

appendixes / appendices The surgeon removed six **appendixes** today.	*Appendixes* are a part of the human body.
The book had three **appendices**.	*Appendices* are sections at the end of a book.

1 indexes / indices	The — are wrong, so the formula is incorrect.
	I've looked up the topic in several — .
2 mediums / media	There were no ghosts at the conference of — this week.
	The — showed great interest in the divorce proceedings.
3 antennas / antennae	The ant-like creatures waved their — vigorously.
	The radio — are used to keep in touch with satellites.
4 formulas / formulae	The mathematical — made no sense to him.
	This government has no magic — for prosperity.

Nouns which do not change

Not all nouns allow you to switch between singular and plural.

- Some nouns are used only in the singular. They include proper nouns (p. 70), noncount nouns (p. 72), and a few others – such as the names of subjects, diseases, and games. Don't be misled by the appearance of the noun: some look as if they have a plural -s ending, but this is deceptive. *Mumps* looks plural, but only when we are joking do we talk of *a mump*. Standard English has:

John was at the party.	not	*Johns were at the party.
Music is relaxing.	not	*Musics are relaxing.
Physics is intriguing.	not	*Physics are intriguing.
Billiards is popular.	not	*Billiards are popular.

- Some nouns are used only in the plural. Here too you must not be misled by the appearance of the noun. Some have an -s ending; others haven't. Standard English has:

Your jeans are on the table.	not	*Your jeans is on the table.
The police are outside.	not	*The police is outside.
The cattle are noisy.	not	*The cattle is noisy.

Two plurals?

A few animal names have two plurals – a regular plural in -s, and a plural without an ending. We can say both *I saw six fish* and *I saw six fishes*. *Shrimp*, *rabbit*, and *duck* are other examples. But there is a difference in meaning. If we are thinking of the animals as individuals, then we use the regular plural. However, if we are thinking of them as wildlife, we use the 'zero' plural. The hunter goes *shooting duck* – not *ducks*. And passers-by at the local pond take their children to *feed the ducks* – never *feed the duck* (unless, of course, the pond contains only one)!

Usage problems

Nouns with a plural in -a cause problems, because their usage has been changing.

- In particular, people have trouble with *data*. This word was once found only as a plural, but it is now often used as a singular, especially in science. Scientists often say *The data is interesting* rather than *The data are interesting*. However, some people prefer to stick to the older pattern.

- There are similar variations with *media*, in the sense of broadcasting and the press. Most people still use the plural form, and say *The media are responsible*; but the singular usage is rapidly growing: *The media is responsible*.

- *Criteria* and *phenomena* are also sometimes heard as singulars: *The criteria is important*, *What an interesting phenomena*. But these usages are unacceptable in Standard English, as are such forms as *criterias*.

Activities

A Decide the number

Choose ten of these nouns ending in *-s* and decide which are used only in the singular (S) and which are used only in the plural (P). Use each one in a sentence.

1 pants	6 economics	11 shingles	16 dominoes
2 darts	7 measles	12 tropics	17 stairs
3 spectacles	8 statistics	13 pyjamas	18 linguistics
4 shears	9 athletics	14 draughts	19 trousers
5 archives	10 lodgings	15 savings	20 credentials

B Correct the errors

A non-native speaker has had difficulty with the choice between singular and plural in these sentences. Turn them into Standard English.

1 *How many people is there in the world today?
2 *Gymnastics need a lot of training.
3 *Have you made an amend for everything you did?
4 *The police wasn't able to do anything about it.
5 *My lodgings is next to the cinema.
6 *Your manners is awful.
7 *The livestock isn't being well looked after.
8 *The odds is worse now that there are more competitors.
9 *She's taken a great pain to get the work in on time.
10 *Vermin causes disease.

C Distinguish the meanings

In these sentences, the nouns can be used either as singular or plural, but with a difference in meaning. Write a commentary to say what this difference is. The first one is done for you.

> Mary Smith's politics are not my cup of tea. / Politics is an interesting subject. In the second sentence, *politics* refers to all aspects of the subject, and every political party; in the first sentence, it refers to only one set of political beliefs.

1 John's writing is awful. / John's writings are not widely known.
2 Her spirit is something to be admired. / The spirits are going to be very expensive.
3 He has very good looks. / He gave me a long hard look.
4 Statistics is a branch of mathematics. / These statistics show that the country is coming out of the recession.
5 Magnetic compasses are needed for navigation. / A compass is useful when you are drawing diagrams in geometry.

21 *People, animals, and things*

In many languages, nouns can be grouped into types, based on the kind of endings they have, or on the way they pattern with other words in the noun phrase. For example, in German, singular nouns preceded by *der* ('the') form one type, called **masculine**. Those preceded by *die* ('the') form another type, called **feminine**. And those preceded by *das* ('the') form a third type, called **neuter**. This kind of grouping is known as **grammatical gender**.

English has no grammatical gender. Words are not masculine or feminine or neuter. But English does have ways of distinguishing between nouns which refer to **animate** (living) beings and those which refer to **inanimate** (non-living) entities. Animate beings can be divided into **personal** (people) and **non-personal** (animals). And in both cases the **male** sex can be distinguished, linguistically, from the **female** sex. This kind of grouping is known as **natural gender**.

The chief words showing these differences are the pronouns (see p. 128), especially *he, she, it, who,* and *which.* Look at these sentences:

> Here is a **box**. **It** is the box **which** was left in the house.
> Here is a **man**. **He** is the man **who** was left in the house.

It / *which* show that *box* is an inanimate noun. *He* / *who* show that *man* is animate.

Personal and non-personal

- Personal animate nouns refer to males / females, and pattern with *he* / *she* / *who*.
  He is the **man who** stayed. **She** is the **woman who** stayed.
  In many cases, you cannot tell the gender from the noun: a *cousin, doctor,* or *artist* could be either *she* or *he.* By contrast, a few nouns show their gender through their ending. In particular, nouns with an *-ess* suffix are always female (*tigress, princess*). However, this ending is less popular these days, because of the movement for sexual equality. Aircraft stewards and stewardesses are now *flight attendants.*

- Non-personal animate nouns refer to animals. Most take *it* and *which*:
  Look at that **camel**. **It**'s the one **which** I saw yesterday.
  But animals can be *he* or *she* if they have a special place in human society, such as dogs and guinea pigs. There may even be separate words for male and female: *dog* / *bitch*. But we do not usually distinguish the sex of lower animals, such as ants and cod – mainly because it isn't easy to tell which is which.

An exception
Non-personal or inanimate nouns can be *she* or *he*, when you think of them in an intimate way. *She* is usually used for countries, cars, ships, and pets.
> Isn't she a beauty?   Britain has increased her exports.

If you want to be rude, you can do the opposite – call a person you don't like *it.*

Activities

A Fill the blanks

Fill the blanks in these sentences with pronouns which match the gender of the noun. Use *he*, *she*, or *it* for the first blank, and *who* or *which* for the second. Note that in some examples you have a choice.

1 I like this ring. — was a gift — my cousin gave me.
2 That's a picture of my Uncle Tom. — 's the one — came on holiday with us.
3 Jane's training to be a doctor. And — 's the one — hated the sight of blood!
4 What about my suggestion? —'s a solution — I think will work.
5 Here's a map of Japan. —'s a country — I'd very much like to visit.
6 Look at that yacht! Isn't — a boat — you'd love to sail in!
7 Have you thought of my niece? I think —'s a person — would be good at the job.
8 Jane's awake. —'s hungry again! I've never met a baby — eats so much!
9 There's the bride. — looks gorgeous, but I've never seen anyone — looks so nervous.
10 We have a guest staying with us. —'s someone — has stayed once before.

B Relate male and female

Here are some nouns showing male and female gender. Match the related forms.

MALE: buck   nephew   bull   cock   dog   gander
        hero   ram   monk   stallion   tiger
FEMALE: ewe   tigress   heroine   doe   nun   cow
        bitch   mare   hen   niece   goose

Can you think of other pairs of words related by gender?

C Avoid sexism

Here are some announcements in which the choice of noun seems to be restricted to one sex only. Rewrite them so that people of either sex could be involved. The first one is done for you. Beware: sometimes you may need to change the structure of the sentence as well.

The postmen are on strike. → The postal workers are on strike.

1 We need to elect a chairman.
2 Who's going to be our spokesman?
3 There's a very strict foreman on the third floor.
4 Who was the cameraman on that film?
5 There are jobs for usherettes at the cinema.
6 I want to be a fireman.
7 There are holiday jobs for stewardesses on the boats.
8 We have four dinner ladies on duty at our school.
9 Would you like a job as a travelling salesman?
10 There's a seminar for businessmen in the Town Hall.

22 *Apostrophe* s

In many languages, nouns have endings which show how a noun relates to other nouns, or how the noun phrase is being used within a clause – such as whether it is acting as subject or object. The set of endings is called the **case** system. English does not have a complex case system, like the ones which are found in Latin or German. English has only two cases: a **common** case, where the noun has no inflectional ending, and the **genitive**.

The genitive case is made by adding an *-s* to the the noun. In writing, with singular nouns, this appears with a preceding apostrophe:

> the doctor → the doctor's bags   the hostage → the hostage's release

With regular plural nouns, an *-s* ending is already there, so the apostrophe goes at the end:

> the doctors → the doctors' bags   the hostages → the hostages' release

Irregular plural nouns simply add an *'s*: *the men's room, the children's play*. But look out for spelling changes: *the family's concern* → *the families' concern*. In the first example, there is only one family; in the second example, there are several families.

In speech, there is no difference in sound between *doctors, doctor's*, and *doctors'*. You have to rely on the context to understand what is being said.

The chief meaning of the genitive case is **possession**. If you have an auntie and a friend, and you want to show that one belongs to the other, you use the genitive.

> my auntie's friend (= 'the friend of my auntie')
> my friend's auntie (= 'the auntie of my friend')

But the case is used to express other meanings too – for example, it can express a period of time: *ten days' leave* (= 'the leave lasts for ten days'). And beware the meanings which hide beneath the surface. *Sally's application* and *Sally's release* both seem to be the same kind of phrase; but they are very different in meaning. In *Sally's application*, it is Sally who is doing the action – 'Sally applied'. In *Sally's release*, it is Sally who is affected by the action – someone released her.

Some exceptions

Not all nouns add a genitive ending. Sometimes the only signal is an apostrophe.

- If you have a Greek name of more than one syllable, and it ends in *-s*, people avoid the tongue-twister. They say *Socrates' thoughts*, not **Socrates's thoughts*.

- Other names can also be affected. Some people prefer *Dickens' novels* because it is easier to say than *Dickens's novels*. And *Jesus' ideas* are more likely than *Jesus's ideas*. But usage varies.

82

Activities

A Add an apostrophe

Decide whether these sentences contain an example of the genitive case with a singular or a plural noun, and add an apostrophe in the right place. The first one is done for you.

1 I've just been talking to the ships captain. → ship's captain
2 Janes clothes are on the table in the hall.
3 After it was hurt, the dogs barking could be heard for miles.
4 This form needs your parents consent.
5 Do you like Robert Burns poetry?
6 She's had three weeks absence from school.
7 It was a lovely summers day.
8 The flies movements were very erratic.
9 The doctors problem is whether they should start using the vaccine.
10 Everyone welcomed the hostages release. The men were in good health.

B Add a noun

In these sentences, the noun following the genitive has been left out, as the context makes it obvious what kind of noun should be there. Add an appropriate noun, as in the first example.

1 Let's all meet at Esther's. → Esther's house
2 I'm staying at my aunt's.
3 This year's final was better than last year's.
4 I buy my clothes at Smith's.
5 They were married in St Paul's.
6 I've just been to the chemist's.
7 We'll eat at Joe's.
8 My bike is faster than Jean's.
9 Mary's was the best answer.
10 I'm going to the doctor's.

C Decide the direction of action

- Work out whether the underlying meaning of these genitive constructions is one of the noun 'doing an action' (D) or being 'affected by an action' (A). Show the meaning like this:

    the family's interest → The family is interested in something. (D)

1 my friends' agreement   3 the MPs' election   5 Mary's employment
2 the engine's explosion   4 the train's arrival   6 the teacher's appointment

- Try this activity the other way round. Begin with a sentence, and turn it into a genitive construction, like this:

    The court released the prisoner. → the prisoner's release (A)

1 The army defeated the enemy.   3 They decided to close the company.
2 Mike suggested a solution.   4 The miners decided to fight.

The of-genitive

There is another way of expressing genitive meanings, and that is to use a construction introduced by *of*:

> the ship's name = the name of the ship

How can you decide which to use – or doesn't it matter?

Often, it doesn't. The two constructions have exactly the same meaning, and the only difference lies in the rhythm. (Of course, it can be very useful to have a choice of this kind available, especially if you are writing poetry, and you need a construction to suit the rhythm of the line.)

But not all nouns are like this. Personal nouns tend to take the genitive ending. Inanimate nouns tend to take the *of*-construction. And often the alternatives are ungrammatical. Compare:

> I've got Fred's book.   not   *I've got the book of Fred.
> That is part of the problem.   not   *That is the problem's part.

The apostrophe

The apostrophe did not become widespread in English until the 17th century, and until about 150 years ago there was a great deal of uncertainty about how it should be used. Printers and grammarians tried to lay down rules, but these rules could not always be made to work neatly. For example, you might think it logical for such words as *hers*, *ours*, and *its* to have an apostrophe, because these words express possession; but they do not. We write:

> The parcel is Mary's.   not   *The parcel is Marys.
> The parcel is hers.   not   *The parcel is her's.

The English writing system has picked up many curiosities of this kind over the centuries, and they are now part of Standard English.

Usage varies enormously over the apostrophe in public signs. Some businesses and place names keep it in (the London tube station is called *St Paul's*); some leave it out (as in *Woolworths* and *Boots*). The fashion in modern signwriting is to leave it out, to avoid signs looking cluttered.

But there has been no change in the basic use of the apostrophe, where it shows the difference between a plural noun and the two genitive uses of a noun.

> the dentists   (no apostrophe = plural)
> the dentist's equipment   (apostrophe before = genitive singular)
> the dentists' equipment   (apostrophe after = genitive plural)

If you see such notices as *WE SELL SHEPHERDS PIE'S*, the writer hasn't learned these rules, and runs the risk of being criticized by people who have.

(English also has another use for the apostrophe: this is described on p. 158.)

Activities

A Choose a genitive

Decide which is the more acceptable way of expressing the genitive with the following nouns. In some cases, the *'s* ending is more likely; in others, it is the construction with *of*. Write them out like this:

house	front → the front of the house	*the house's front
Mary	book → Mary's book	*the book of Mary

1 Esther	school	6 balance	trade
2 summer	day	7 girls	school
3 declaration	independence	8 part	problem
4 Noah	ark	9 dance	seven veils
5 age	revolution	10 Duke	York

B Make corrections

- These sign writers have obviously not learned the rules governing how we use the apostrophe in English. Correct their work. (Look out for spelling changes.)

1 Post no bill's.	6 We repair watch's.
2 Babies bonnets, third floor.	7 Lambs liver.
3 Fish and chip's for sale.	8 Postcard's.
4 New potato's now in.	9 New family's this way.
5 Danger. Horse's crossing.	10 Lifts'.

- Carry out your own survey of apostrophe errors in your locality.

C Explain the choices

Here are some lines from William Blake's 'London' which contain genitive constructions. In each case, the alternative way of forming a genitive is theoretically possible. In a group, identify the genitives and discuss why the poet has made the choices he has.

> In every cry of every Man,
> In every Infant's cry of fear,
> In every voice, in every ban,
> The mind-forg'd manacles I hear.
>
> How the Chimney-sweeper's cry
> Every black'ning Church appalls;
> And the hapless Soldier's sigh
> Runs in blood down Palace walls.

23 *Building up noun phrases*

A noun phrase is a string of words which all depend on the noun in some way. The noun is the most important word in a noun phrase. It tells you what the noun phrase is basically about.

To build up a noun phrase from a single noun, you can add words before it:

Bicycles	will be there.
Those bicycles	will be there.
Those new bicycles	will be there.
Several of those new, expensive racing bicycles	will be there.

You can add words after it:

Bicycles with special pedals	will be there.
Bicycles with special pedals which you can take abroad	will be there.

Or, of course, you can do both at once:

Those bicycles with special pedals   will be there.

Noun phrases can become long, complex, and ambiguous, if you don't keep them under control. Here's a monster example, where the noun phrase goes on and on.

(I'm going to sell) all those brand new expensive racing bicycles with special pedals and the stripes on the crossbar which reminded me of the carvings from Africa which we're storing in the garage down Smith Street that belongs to Uncle Jim.

Some people do talk like that! But they can easily lose their listeners. And if you want your readers to understand you, it would be very unwise to write like that.

The head of the noun phrase

The noun is the chief word, or **head**, of the noun phrase. Here are some noun phrases, with their heads highlighted:

A <u>*cat*</u> *with black spots* ran across *the main <u>road</u>* in front of *a big <u>lorry</u>*.

Note that the first noun phrase has another noun phrase inside it: *black spots* is telling you something extra about *a cat*. So how do we know that *cat* is the head, rather than *spots*?

- The verb tells us that something was running across a road. Spots don't run. Cats do. So *cat* must be the word which governs the verb *run*.

- *Was* is one of those verbs which agrees with the subject in number (see p. 52). It is a singular form of the verb, so it requires a singular subject. *Cat* is a singular noun. *Spots* is a plural noun. So *cat* must go with *was*.

You need to think like this when you see a 'noun phrase inside a noun phrase'.

Activities

A Find the head

Find the head of the noun phrase in each of the following examples.

1 A brilliant idea came to her.
2 The branches of the tree were alight.
3 They saw a bright yellow light.
4 I know the answer.
5 I met several interesting people.

6 There's a knife with a red handle.
7 That's the person I was expecting.
8 We fell over on the slippery wet path.
9 Who's the king of the castle?
10 Each of his entries won something.

B Identify the noun phrases

Here are the opening lines of Bernard Mac Laverty's short story, 'Across the Street'. Identify the noun phrases and write them out in a list, underlining the heads.

> *On summer evenings she used to practise the flute in front of a music-stand with the window open. She played with verve, her elbows high, her body moving to the tempo of the music. Every time she stopped she flicked her shoulder-length hair with her hand and, with a little backward-shaking motion of her head to make sure it was out of her way, she would begin again. In the pauses of her playing Mr Keogh could hear the slow hooting of pigeons.*

There are four examples of 'a noun phrase inside a noun phrase'. Which are they?

C Expand the noun phrases

- Add some words of your own to each of the noun phrases in your list, trying to make them fit in with the story. Experiment with putting some words in front of the head or after the head. For example, *a music-stand* might become *a broken music-stand* or *a music-stand with a broken leg*.

- In a group, compare your versions, and discuss what happens to the story. Do the extra details add interest, or are they a distraction? Does the story become more difficult to follow, when the noun phrases become larger?

D Compare the styles

Here are two sentences from a science textbook, with the noun phrases highlighted. Compare them with those in the short story. What are the chief differences? Is all science language like this? Look at some other textbooks and find out.

The determination of the age of a terrestrial impact feature may be difficult unless we have **a detailed knowledge of the local geology and its history**.

The optical spectrum of the aurora is characterized by **numerous emission lines and bands from neutral** as well as **ionized and molecular states of hydrogen and oxygen**.

24 *Adding words before a noun*

Consider the difference between the following noun phrases:

> a bicycle   the bicycle   my bicycle   that bicycle   **each bicycle**

Depending on which word goes with *bicycle*, so we know something extra about it. Words like these help us see a noun from a certain point of view. They 'determine' how definite or specific a noun it is, whether a noun is singular or plural, or how many instances of the noun there are. They are therefore called **determiners**.

Determiners

The determiner is a word which always goes in front of a noun. Often, it is the only other word in the noun phrase. Its job is to tell you what kind of noun is in the noun phrase. There are several kinds of noun, as we have seen (p. 70) – common nouns, proper nouns, and others. The determiner decides which kind of noun it is.

Which, whose, and how many?

- *The bicycle* suggests a more definite kind of bicycle than *a bicycle*. If you say, *I can see a bicycle*, you need not have seen it before. You're not very definite about which bicycle it is. But if you say *I can see the bicycle*, it must be one you've been expecting. It's a more definite notion. It's for this reason that *a* is called the **indefinite article** and *the* is called the **definite article**.

- *That* suggests something being pointed out, some distance away. It contrasts with *this*, which suggests something a bit nearer. *That bicycle* is further away than *this bicycle*. Similarly, *those bicycles* are further away than *these bicycles*.

- *My* adds the idea of possession, as do *your, his, her, its, our,* and *their*.

- *Either* and *neither* give us a choice of two. The first is positive: if you say *I'll take either bicycle*, you will end up with a bicycle. The second is negative: if you say *I'll take neither bicycle*, you won't.

- *Some, any, each, every,* and *enough* all tell us that there must be a number of bicycles. *Some* usually appears in a positive sentence; *any* in a negative or questioning sentence. Note especially that we say:
  > I can see **some** *bicycles*.   not   *I can't see **some** *bicycles*.
  > I can't see **any** *bicycles*.   not   *I can see **any** *bicycles*.

  If we use *each*, we are thinking of the bicycles one at a time: *Each bicycle has been mended*. If we use *every*, we are thinking of the bicycles all together: *Every bicycle has been damaged*.

- *What bicycle* raises the question of whether there is a bicycle there at all. *No bicycle* definitely tells us there isn't.

Activities

A Find the determiner

Underline the determiner in the noun phrases in these sentences. (Two examples are not Standard English. Find them, and turn them into Standard English.)

1 My bike is older than your bike.
2 Have you seen the latest fashions?
3 I'd love some fried eggs.
4 All your books are on the table.
5 Either road will get you to the hotel.
6 I can't see no stars.
7 Each member will carry a flag.
8 The lake is behind that hill.
9 I don't have any time.
10 I've read them books.

B Match the meanings

Match one of the determiners on the left with one of the meanings on the right.

1 I can see that car.
2 I can see some cars.
3 I can see no car.
4 I can see every car.
5 I can see each car.
6 I can see the car.
7 Which car was that?
8 I can see neither car.
9 I can see a car.
10 I can see your car.

A I'm not talking about any particular car.
B I'm talking about the car I already mentioned.
C I'm talking about a car which is owned by someone.
D I'm talking about a car some distance away.
E I'm talking about two cars which I don't want.
F I'm talking about a number of cars in a car park.
G I'm talking about all the cars in a car park.
H I'm talking about the fact that I can't see a car.
I I'm asking you about the car you saw.
J I'm talking about the individual cars in the car park.

C Fill the blanks

Here is an extract from Robin Jenkins' *The Cone-Gatherers* (Chapter 12), with the determiners omitted. Fill them in, then discuss why some are used more than others.

> As Mr. Tulloch walked through — wood to visit — cone-gatherers, he stopped to look at — beech split almost to — ground by yesterday's lightning. — freshness of — tortured wood was for him — most powerful of all — fragrances — sunny windy morning. He lingered beside — tremendous tree, pitying it. Anyone sheltering under it during — storm would have been squashed like — wood-louse under — thumb; and anyone clinging to — upper branches would have been sizzled like — flea in — fire. Before he moved on, he plucked up — handful of old leaves still damp from yesterday's deluge, and scattered them in — air.

D Carry out a determiner survey

- Make a collection of film or book titles which contain determiners (e.g. *The Fly*), and find out which determiners turn up most often.

- In a group, discuss what happens if you change the determiners (e.g. *Some Flies*).

Describing words

You can add several other words between the determiner and the noun, and they all do the same sort of job – giving extra information about the noun. We can call them **describing** words. Usually, noun phrases contain just one or two describing words – but it is very easy to build up some very long sequences.

DETERMINER		NOUN
the	fat	cat
my	creamy, minty, chewy, buttery, smooth, tasty ...	chocolates

- The commonest type of describing word is the adjective (see p. 136), along with any words which strengthen the adjective's meaning, such as *very* or *quite*:

    a <u>lovely</u> day   a <u>quite large</u> table   a <u>very interesting</u> clock

You can use adjectives to build up long noun phrases:

    a small, circular table
    a small, circular, expensive table
    a very small, almost circular, remarkably expensive table

- Certain forms of the verb (the **participles**, p. 104) can also be used in an adjective-like way:

    to crumble → a **crumbling** wall   to steal → a **stolen** car

- Some nouns can also be used in an adjective-like way:

    the <u>city</u> street   a <u>tourist</u> spot

Note than when nouns are used like this, they don't behave like nouns any more. We can't turn them into the plural, for example, and say **the cities street* or **a tourists spot*.

Which word order?

When you have a long string of describing words, you have to decide on the order to put them in. Adjectives with a very general or strengthening meaning, such as *nice* or *entire*, tend to come first, immediately after the determiner. Noun-like words, such as *garden* or *American*, tend to come last. The other adjectives come in between.

On this basis, the following word order sounds very natural.

    I've bought those nice big red garden chairs.

Are any other orders possible? *I've bought those red garden big chairs* isn't. Nor is **I've bought those garden big red chairs*. It makes an interesting grammar experiment to try out different word orders, and see which are possible, which are impossible, and which change the meaning or emphasis of the sentence in some way.

Activities

A Distinguish types of describing word

Look at these noun phrases, and decide whether the describing words are adjectives (A), verb forms being used in an adjective-like way (V), or nouns being used in an adjective-like way (N).

1 an intelligent reply	5 an embarrassing situation	9 a shining light
2 that broken toy	6 my beautiful launderette	10 the town centre
3 the shop front	7 a special relationship	
4 the largest amount	8 every convicted criminal	

B Find an acceptable order

Here are some noun phrases containing strings of describing words in an ungrammatical order. Turn them into an order which sounds natural.

1 *teak tall six wardrobes
2 *the very comedy British best films
3 *some French hot onion nice soup
4 *a colourful cardboard large container
5 *those fine wooden red old door knobs

C Discuss the role of describing words

Here is the opening of Thomas Hardy's 'Fellow-Townsmen' (from *Wessex Tales*).

• Make a list of the noun phrases which contain describing words.

• How important are these words in the passage? Try leaving them out, and see what happens to the meaning of the sentence. In a group, discuss why some describing words can easily be left out, whereas others cannot.

> *The shepherd on the east hill could shout out lambing intelligence to the shepherd on the west hill, over the intervening town chimneys, without great inconvenience to his voice, so nearly did the steep pastures encroach upon the burghers' backyards. And at night it was possible to stand in the very midst of the town and hear from their native paddocks on the lower levels of greensward the mild lowings of the farmer's heifers, and the profound, warm blowings of breath in which those creatures indulge. But the community which had jammed itself in the valley thus flanked formed a veritable town, with a real mayor and corporation, and a staple manufacture.*

D Carry out a survey

Carry out a survey of the extent to which describing words are used in the titles of books or television programmes, e.g. *Blind* Date, The *Chart* Show, *Great* Expectations. Is their use influenced by the subject-matter? For example, would you expect more describing words in works of fiction or of non-fiction?

Counting the noun

There are some other kinds of word which we can add before the noun. These are used to express the important idea of 'how much' or 'how many'. We can call them **quantity** words. They are often used alongside determiners, which also help to express the idea of quantity.

- Several quantity words occur before a determiner, at the very beginning of the noun phrase:

<u>all</u> the cars   <u>both</u> the cars   <u>half</u> the cars
<u>twice</u> the cost   <u>such</u> a fuss   <u>a quarter</u> the amount

Some of them can be followed by *of*: *all of the cars*, *a quarter of the amount*.

- Several quantity words occur immediately after a determiner. The commonest examples are the numerals. Numerals such as *one (1)*, *two (2)*, and *three (3)* are called the **cardinal numerals**, because they are the basic type of numeral. Numerals such as *first*, *second*, and *third* are called the **ordinal numerals**, because they show the order of things in a series.

cardinal numerals: my **three** cats   the **50** sheep
ordinal numerals: my **third** cat   her **50th** birthday

Other quantity words include *much, many, few, little*, and *several*. They are also often followed by *of*: *many people | many of the people*; *three cats | three of the cats*.

You can of course have quantity words going before and after the determiner at the same time, as these examples show:

QUANTITY WORDS	DETERMINER	QUANTITY WORDS	NOUN
	the		bicycles
all	the		bicycles
all	the	50	bicycles
both of	my	last two	bicycles

Words with different jobs to do

When you are studying noun phrases, you will notice that some words turn up in different places. This doesn't apply to *the, a, every, my*, and the other possessive words. All they do is go before a noun. They are determiners only.

But look at the ways in which this word can be used:
(1) I bought <u>some</u> apples.   (2) I bought <u>some</u> of the apples.
(3) I bought <u>some</u>.
In (1), *some* is being used immediately before the noun, as a determiner.
In (2), it is being used **in front of** a determiner, as a quantity word.
And in (3) there is no noun there at all. *Some* is standing in for a noun – it is a **pronoun** (p. 128). You will find that *this, each, either*, and several other determiners can be used in this way.

Activities

A Find the quantity words

Find the quantity words in the noun phrases in these sentences.

1 I've put all the suitcases in the boot.
2 She's got over a hundred CDs.
3 Several of his recent records have been flops.
4 The first thing I want to do is buy two new brake pads.
5 Half of the property belongs to Sarah.
6 Can I have a little more coffee?
7 There have been many interested customers coming into the shop.
8 First prize, Emma; second prize, Ken; third prize, Hilary.
9 Few people know the answer.
10 You can't fool all of the people all of the time.

B Investigate the use of quantity words

● Here is an extract from a report on a laboratory experiment. Identify the quantity words used in the report.

> *In the first study, we examined three situations in which six children had to guess the location of a ball. In the first situation, all the children were on the same side of a wall, and all of them shared one map. In the second situation, half of the children were given their own maps. And in the third situation, only one child was given a map. They were then given a time frame of five minutes to complete the task.*

● In a group, discuss why there are so many quantity words in this kind of writing. Get hold of some teaching materials from science classes, and see whether they are common there too.

C Distinguish the different uses of a word

Decide whether the highlighted words in these sentences are being used as a determiner (D), a quantity word going before a determiner (Q), or a pronoun (P).

1 **Some** friends came round last night.
2 I didn't buy **any**.
3 **This** didn't surprise me.
4 **The** answer, **my** friend, is blowing in **the** wind.
5 **Either** will get you there on time.
6 They gave **each of** the players **an** extra five pounds.
7 **Each** player was delighted.
8 I think **these** cherries are a bit off.
9 Let me have **some**, will you?
10 **Our** cats will need **both of** the injections.

25 *Adding words after a noun*

You can also add words after the noun in a noun phrase. There are three main ways of doing this, and each way involves a special kind of construction.

- The commonest way uses a string of words consisting of a preposition (see p. 144) followed by a noun phrase (a **prepositional phrase**):

    (I own) the car **in the street**.   (I hear) a man **on the radio**.

- You can put in extra detail by adding a verb:

    (I own) the car **parked in**   (I hear) a man **singing on**
    the street.   **the radio**.

This turns the string of words into a simple type of clause. These clauses are like those on p. 30, but they have no subject, and the helping verbs are missing.

- You can put in still more detail by adding the helping verbs, so that you can now talk about such matters as the time of the action:

    (I own) the car **which I parked**   (I hear) a man **who is singing**
    in the street.   **on the radio**.

Now the verbs are fully present, expressing past or present time, and there is a subject (*I* or *who*). Clauses of this kind are called **relative clauses**. They can usually be easily identified by their opening word (such as *who*, *which*, or *whom*), but when the linking word is *that*, it is often left out. We can say both *Look at the book that I found* and *Look at the book I found*.

Beware ambiguity

Often, more than one of these three constructions is used at the same time:
    (I own) the car / with a red roof / parked outside / which you liked.
But sequences of this kind can become unwieldy, and they must be used very carefully to avoid being ambiguous. Compare these two sentences:
    (I can see) the lady / in the corner / looking at the picture.
    (I can see) the lady / looking at the picture / in the corner.
In the first case, the lady is in the corner. In the second case, it could be the picture – but it might just be the lady. And in this example, it's impossible to say who's wearing the coat:
    (I can see) the lady with a man in a red coat.
In particular, try to avoid sentences which permit a bizarre interpretation:
    (I can see) a man / in a hat / walking down the street.
The sentence isn't really ambiguous, because we all know that hats don't walk. But because you can read in that meaning, it might cause an unintended smile. To get out of trouble, try expressing the sentence in a different way.
    That man walking down the street is wearing a hat.

Activities

A Find the constructions

Find the constructions which follow the noun in the noun phrase. Identify any which are prepositional phrases (PP) or relative clauses (RC). The first one is done for you.

1 Can you see the number on the front door? → on the front door (PP)
2 The picture on the sideboard was a present.
3 I can hear footsteps ringing on the pavement.
4 That's the man who came to see you yesterday.
5 What will you do with the prize which you won in the lottery?
6 I'll store the furniture left outside.
7 The cat with the ginger stripe is my favourite.
8 I like the scarf Jim gave me.
9 I prefer the scarf with the red stripes.
10 I bought this scarf reduced in the sale.

B Remove the ambiguity

These sentences probably don't mean what they seem to be saying. Rewrite them to get rid of the ambiguity.

1 She went to town with her spaniel in her best jeans.
2 The car just missed a mother and baby who was pushing a pram.
3 A tall man was dancing with a pair of glasses.
4 I've just read a book about a holiday village called *Murder*.
5 Our school trip saw the Tower of London sailing down the river.
6 The lady saw a cat in front of her driving a taxi.
7 The children watched the dolphins, wrapped up well to keep out the cold.
8 I followed the fish with a camera.
9 The children were soaked by the hosepipe running around the garden.
10 Staggering wildly, the vicar spoke to the drunk.

C Turn before into after

These sentences all contain describing words before a noun. Turn the describing words into a construction which comes after the noun. The first one is done for you.

I found a very beautiful picture. → I found a picture which was very beautiful.

1 Joe slipped on the frozen path.
2 I had to buy a very expensive suit for the wedding.
3 Look at that happy, chubby-cheeked baby.
4 I've just seen a prize-winning film.
5 They'll be staying at their Riviera flat next week.

26 *The noun phrase: a summary*

Most noun phrases have a very simple structure:

the dog   my old house   the car in the garage

But it is possible to build up a noun phrase so that it becomes long and complex:

all those horrible, red, wooden chairs with broken arms lying in the garage

These monsters can always be analysed into three basic parts: the head noun; what goes before this noun; and what goes after it. Work out the structure in steps:

1 **Find the head.** In the above sentence, it is *chairs*.
2 **Find the determiner.** In that sentence, it is *those*.
3 **Find any describing words.** In that sentence, they are *horrible, red, wooden*.
4 **Find any other quantity words.** In that sentence there is *all*.
5 **Find any constructions following the noun.** In that sentence there are two: *with broken arms* and *lying in the garage*.

Noun phrases within noun phrases

You will often find noun phrases hiding within the constructions that follow a head noun. In the above, there are two: *broken arms* consists of a noun preceded by a describing word; *the garage* consists of a noun preceded by a determiner.

These are 'junior' noun phrases inside the 'senior' noun phrase! Each of them could of course build into a complex construction in its own right – but you have to be careful, because it is easy for a sentence to get out of control when you let all the noun phrases grow. Look at the sentence with just one of the 'junior' noun phrases expanded. It is now much more difficult to take it all in.

(I'm going to sell) those horrible, red, wooden chairs with broken arms lying in the old garage with blue windows in Smith Street.

Carrying on a noun phrase for ever

Here is a famous type of sentence in which you can make a noun phrase grow and grow – and in theory continue for ever. Each sentence ends: . . . *who lived in the house that Jack built.* Each stage has an extra construction with a new noun phrase junior to the one before.
This is **the man** . . .
This is the man who owns **the dog** . . .
This is the man who owns the dog which chased **the cat** . . .
This is the man who owns the dog which chased the cat which worried **the rat** . . .
It is just about possible to follow the meaning of this sentence because each additional part has the same sort of structure and rhythm.

Activities

A Construct a table

Construct a table which contains a place for all the possible parts of a noun phrase, like this:

QUANTITY WORDS	DETERMINER	QUANTITY WORDS	DESCRIBING WORDS	HEAD	FOLLOWING CONSTRUCTIONS
all	the	three	American	visitors	in raincoats

Now examine each of the following noun phrases, and decide which words go under which heading. Leave out the words in brackets. Not all of the headings will be found in each noun phrase, of course.

1 (There was) a sudden sound of footsteps.
2 Both of their back windows (were broken).
3 (He saw) two faint black marks left by his shoes.
4 (She bought) an interesting jigsaw puzzle.
5 The weird shape of the crane (loomed up ahead of them).
6 Several of the new car parts (are missing).
7 (It was) a very dark night.
8 (They had) wet leaves clinging to their feet.
9 Some of the daily newspapers (had been lost).
10 (It's) that brilliant new release which got to number one last week.

B Create noun phrases

Create two noun phrases to fit each of the following formulas:

DETERMINER + THREE DESCRIBING WORDS + NOUN
DETERMINER + QUANTITY WORD + TWO DESCRIBING WORDS + NOUN
QUANTITY WORD + DETERMINER + NOUN + RELATIVE CLAUSE
QUANTITY WORD + DETERMINER + QUANTITY WORD + NOUN

C Attach one noun phrase to another

Here are some pairs of noun phrases. Construct a sentence in which the second noun phrase is attached to the noun in the first noun phrase, so that it becomes the 'junior' partner. The first example is done for you. Note that there could be more than one solution, as here:

> a town + Leeds → I live in a town near Leeds. or I live in a town which is near Leeds.

1 a hot Sunday + July
2 a crew + four people
3 the fridge + the kitchen
4 that old desk + the second-hand shop
5 the questions + the exam
6 all the cows + the farmyard
7 the relief + her face
8 memories + our last holidays
9 relationships + people
10 a chief officer + a ship

An example

'Don't Panic' is the slogan of *The Hitch-Hiker's Guide to the Galaxy* by Douglas Adams – an appropriate piece of advice for anyone studying English grammar. Here's an extract from that book, with the noun phrases highlighted. Note that half of the words belong to noun phrases.

> **The Heart of Gold** fled on silently through **the night of space**, now on **conventional photon drive**. **Its crew of four** were ill at ease knowing that they had been brought together not out of **their own volition** or by **simple coincidence**, but by **some curious perversion of physics** – as if **relationships between people** were susceptible to **the same laws that governed the relationships between atoms and molecules**.
>
> As **the ship's artificial night** closed in they were each grateful to retire to **separate cabins** and try to rationalize **their thoughts**.
>
> **Trillian** couldn't sleep.

Look out for the following features:

- In *Its crew of four* the author has left out the head noun in the prepositional phrase, because it is obvious what is meant – *people* or *travellers*.

- *The ship's artificial night* has a genitive noun (see p. 82), *ship's*, as a describing word before the head noun, *night*. *Ship* could itself have words attached to it, of course. However, if you are constructing sentences like this, make sure you put these words in the right place: *the huge ship's artificial light* means something very different from *the ship's huge artificial light*.

- There are some noun phrases which have another noun phrase attached to them, as part of a prepositional phrase. In most cases, this 'junior' noun phrase consists of just the head word: *the Heart of **Gold***, *the night of **space***.

- The following noun phrase has quite a complicated structure: there are noun phrases inside noun phrases inside noun phrases!

    the same **laws** that governed the relationships between atoms and molecules

    the **relationships** between atoms and molecules

    atoms   **molecules**

At the 'most senior level', the head of the noun phrase is *laws*. At the 'second level', in the construction following *laws*, there is another noun phrase, whose head is *relationships*. And at the 'third level', within the construction following *relationships*, there are two other noun phrases, linked by *and*, each consisting of just one word.

All this grammar in 11 words! And you probably read the phrase without even thinking about it. Examples of this kind show just how much grammar you already know. And when you have learned to analyse examples like this, you can prove it!

Activities

Create a noun phrase generator

1 Form a group of six. Think of a noun phrase as a sequence of 'slots', as on p. 97. Each person is made the collector of material for one slot. You should have:

- a collector of nouns – both singular and plural
- a collector of determiners
- a collector of quantity words that go at the beginning of the noun phrase
- a collector of quantity words that go after the determiner
- a collector of describing words
- a collector of constructions that go after the noun

One of the class acts as scribe, to write down on record sheets the noun phrases generated. One sheet is headed **grammatical**; the other **ungrammatical**.

2 Each collector finds 10 examples which belong to a slot, but doesn't show the others what they are. They then write their examples down on separate slips of paper.

3 The group forms a line, in the order of the slots in the noun phrase. It then starts generating noun phrases, from left to right. Each person puts a piece of paper down, until there is a sequence of six. The group then shows the sequence to the rest of the class.

4 The class has to decide whether the noun phrase is grammatical. If it is, the scribe writes it on the **grammatical** record sheet exactly as it is. If it isn't, the scribe writes it on the other sheet, and adds an asterisk. If the class can't agree, take a vote.

5 When the group has used up all its examples, the class sees how many grammatical noun phrases it has generated. The group then has to take the ungrammatical ones, work out where they have gone wrong, and make them grammatical. The scribe writes down each change. The activity ends when all the noun phrases are judged grammatical. (If you want, you can turn this activity into a competition, to see which group takes the fewest steps to generate ten grammatical noun phrases.)

An example

One group generated these sequences:

| all | my | thirteen | ridiculous | chickens | in the lighthouse |
| half | a | many | lovely | toadstool | which I stroked |

The first example is a bit strange, but the class judged it grammatical. The second example had an asterisk slapped on it straight away, and the group had to correct it in two steps:

  1 They changed *toadstool* from singular to plural.
  2 They changed *a* to *the*.

Some members wanted to change *half* to *half of* and *many* to a numeral, but they were outvoted.

Verbs and Verb Phrases

4 Verbs and verb phrases

A verb phrase is the name of the construction which can appear as the verb (V) element within a clause (p. 34). In its simplest form, it consists of just a verb.

The crowds <u>**left**</u>.	That clown <u>**was**</u> funny.	Oil <u>**floats**</u> on water.
<u>S</u> <u>V</u>	<u>S</u> <u>V</u> <u>C</u>	<u>S</u> <u>V</u> <u>A</u>

But we can make a verb the centre, or **head**, of a string of words, as in the examples below. These verb-based strings are called **verb phrases**.

The contestants	<u>**jumped**</u>.
The contestants	have <u>**jumped**</u>.
The contestants	have been <u>**jumping**</u>.
The contestants	must have been <u>**jumping**</u>.
The contestants	mustn't have been <u>**jumping**</u>.

Despite all the other words in the phrase, each of these sentences is about the same activity: *jumping*.

Part 4 is all about verb phrases. Verb phrases do not show as complex a range of constructions as noun phrases. Most verb phrases are very short, consisting of only two or three words. But these few words express some extremely subtle shades of meaning. Verb phrases really make you think about what it is you're trying to say.

27 *Different kinds of verb*

Two types of verb can occur within the verb phrase.

- The **main verb.** This is the verb which expresses most of the meaning of the verb phrase. It tells you what the verb phrase is about. In the phrase *must have been jumping*, each word contributes something to the meaning, but *jumping* contributes most of all. There is no limit to the number of verbs of this type:

    run   go   look   want   think   find   decide   anticipate

    These verbs convey a wide range of meanings. Some express an action or event, such as *run* and *find*. Some express a mental state or sensation, such as *want* and *look*. Some express a state of being, such as *sleep* or *exist*. People sometimes think of a verb as a 'doing' word. But there are many verbs which do not seem to 'do' anything.

- The 'helping' or **auxiliary verb.** This is a verb which helps the main verb to express important nuances of meaning, such as the time at which an action took place. There are very few auxiliary verbs (see p. 110). They include *am*, *is*, *has*, *did*, *may*, *will*, *shall*, *can*, and *could*.

Doing two jobs

Three important verbs can be used either as main verbs or as auxiliary verbs: the various forms of *be*, *have*, and *do*. Compare these sentences:

    They / are / outside.   They / are going.
     S   V   A   S   V

In the first sentence, *are* is the only verb in the **V** element. It is therefore acting as the main verb. But in the second sentence, there is another verb alongside, *going*. Here, therefore, *are* is acting as an auxiliary verb. The same thing happens here with *has* and *did* in these sentences:

    She / has / a dog.   She / has seen / a dog.
     S   V   O   S   V   O
    They / did / their homework.   They / *did* finish / their homework.
     S   V   O   S   V   O

Look at the ending

You can often tell that a word is a verb by looking at the suffix. There are four important suffixes which form verbs from either nouns or adjectives.

    orchestra + -ate → orchestrate   simple + -ify → simplify
    deaf + -en → deafen   modern + -ize / -ise → modernize / modernise

The spelling *-ize* is standard in American English, and in recent years has been replacing *-ise* in British English. But usage is still mixed.

Activities

A Separate auxiliary and main verbs

Identify the verb phrases, and put them in a table which separates auxiliary verbs and main verbs. Note that some sentences contain more than one verb phrase.

AUXILIARY VERB	MAIN VERB
has	gone

1 My watch has been running slow.
2 I won't be going to the party.
3 I anticipate a very promising future.
4 She must have left by now.
5 I shall have a drink of milk.
6 My glass is empty.
7 They couldn't fix the boiler.
8 I do wish you would stay.
9 Do you know what he said?
10 I have found the book.

B Insert the verbs

In this extract from Gerald Durrell's *Catch me a Colobus* (Chapter 3), all the auxiliary verbs and some of the main verbs have been left out. Fill the gaps.

> *Like any sensible zoo, we — not allow the public to — the animals. This is because they — give them the wrong sort of food, or too much of something that they happen to — particularly, and this — prevent them from — the carefully balanced diet we — worked out for them. For instance, the great apes — go on eating chocolate, rather like children, until they — sick, and then they — refuse their evening meal which — — done them much more good. They — then perhaps develop stomach trouble, and you have a long job curing the complaint that — arisen from wrong feeding. But some of the public who — to the zoo — take the slightest notice of the signs that we have all over the place, saying 'Please — not feed these animals', and continue to — bars of chocolate and other tidbits with gay abandon through the bars of the cages. . . .*

C Add a suffix

These nouns / adjectives can form a verb by adding one of the suffixes listed on the facing page. Find out what the verbs are, then use each one in a sentence.

1 hyphen	2 simple	3 solid	4 deep	5 terror
6 vaccine	7 dead	8 magnet	9 drama	10 damp

D Replace the suffix

Someone has put the wrong suffix on the following verbs. Make corrections.

1 intensize	2 summarify	3 softize	4 originize	5 vandalify
6 scrutinate	7 pollenize	8 loosify	9 pressurify	10 examplize

28 *Regular verbs*

Main verbs are either regular or irregular. The forms of a regular verb can be predicted by the rules of grammar. An irregular verb is one where some of the verb forms are unpredictable, and have to be learned by heart. There are thousands of regular verbs, but under 300 irregular ones.

Regular verb forms

Regular verbs appear in four forms, each of which has a different job to do in the clause.

- The **base form**. This is the form without any endings. It is the form you will find if you look the verb up in a dictionary. Another name for the base form of a verb is the **infinitive form**.

    jump   try   look   discover   remember

- The **-s form**. This is made by adding an *–s* ending to the base form (sometimes with a change in spelling). It is used only in the present tense (p. 114).

    jumps   tries   looks   discovers   panics

- The **-ing form** or **-ing participle**. This is made by adding *–ing* to the base form (often with a spelling change):

    jumping   trying   looking   discovering   panicking

It is chiefly used to stress the idea of an action in progress. *The bear was looking at us* suggests a longer period of time than *The bear looked at us*.

- The **-ed form** or **-ed participle**. This is made by adding *–ed* to the base form (often with a spelling change).

    jumped   tried   looked   discovered   panicked

You will find this form used in several ways. It is used on its own as a way of showing past time: *They jumped*. But it also works along with auxiliary verbs to help express other notions, such as recent action: *They have (just) jumped* (see p. 116).

Why call them participles?

The term **participle** is from Latin grammar. It refers to any forms which can be used either as a verb or in an adjective-like way. Such forms 'take part' or 'participate' in two types of word. You can see this in the following sentences. In the first, the participle form is being used as a verb. In the second, it is being used as a describing word (see p. 90).

He is **racing**.   The house has a **racing** track.
I **parked** the car.   I can see a **parked** car.

Activities

A List entries for a dictionary

Imagine you have to write a dictionary of verbs for foreign learners of English, based on the following extract. You have three tasks to carry out:

- Find all the main verbs in the extract.

- Turn each verb into its base form (if it isn't there already).

- Show that each verb is regular in Standard English by writing four sentences, using (1) the base form, (2) the *-s* form, (3) the *-ing* form, and (4) the *-ed* form.

Write the data out like this:

kicking → kick	BASE	Sarah can kick a ball a long way.
	-S	Smith kicks the ball quickly back to Jones.
	-ING	The horses have been kicking each other.
	-ED	Those boys kicked my sand-castle over.

> *'The train should have reached us by now', exclaimed Mrs Smith pompously, glancing at the clock. 'I shall feel great annoyance if it arrives very late, as we're expected at the hotel before 3 o'clock.' Martin looked unhappy. He rushed across the room, collided with the table, and caused a vase to wobble precariously before it tipped over and crashed onto the hard tiles. 'He behaves like an elephant at times', Mrs Smith observed with a wry smile. 'Terribly sorry', stammered Martin. He picked up the pieces of vase, looking around sheepishly, and placed them carefully on the table, staring hard at them as if he was hoping they would somehow miraculously join together again.*

B Choose the correct forms

In this extract from Richard Carpenter's *Catweazle* (Chapter 3), the regular verbs are shown in their base form in square brackets. Replace them by forms which fit the context, like this: *watch → watched*. (*Adamcos* is Catweazle's magic dagger.)

> *From the bushes, Carrot [watch] with horror as Sam set off with a large axe over his shoulder. There was nothing the boy could do to stop him so, keeping out of sight, he [follow] Sam up to the hen house which stood [rot] away in the corner of Top Field.*
>
> *Sam [try] the door but it wouldn't open because Catweazle had [tie] it shut with a piece of twine. 'That's funny,' [mutter] Sam, [tug] at the handle. Hearing Sam outside, Catweazle [struggle] into his damp robe as quickly as he could. Sam [pull] harder and as the twine finally [snap], he [stagger] back and sat down.*
>
> *Catweazle [poke] his head out of the door and the two of them [stare] at each other.*
> *'I'm nuts', [mutter] Sam unhappily. 'I ought to be [lock] up.'*
> *'I am invisible, invisible', [quaver] Catweazle, [wave] Adamcos.*
> *'I wish you was', [groan] Sam getting unsteadily to his feet.*

29 *Irregular verbs*

Irregular verbs make their *-s* form and their *-ing* form by adding an ending to the base, in the same way as regular verbs. But they have either an unpredictable past tense, or an unpredictable *-ed* participle form, or both. Many irregular verbs therefore appear in *five* forms, not four. Compare regular *jump* with irregular *speak*.

BASE FORM	–S FORM	–ING FORM	–ED FORM USED AS PAST TENSE	–ED FORM USED AS PARTICIPLE
jump	She jumps	I'm jumping	I jumped	I've jumped
speak	She speaks	I'm speaking	I spoke	I've spoken

- Most irregular verbs change the vowel of the base forms:

  meet → met   take → took   speak → spoken   see → saw

Sometimes there is a change of consonant as well:

  keep → kept   teach → taught   sell → sold

- The *-ed* ending is never used in a regular way. Sometimes there is a completely different ending, such as *-n* or *-en*. Sometimes there is just a change of consonant. Sometimes there is no ending at all.

DIFFERENT ENDING	take → taken	see → seen
CONSONANT CHANGE	have → had	send → sent
NO ENDING	cut → cut	shut → shut

You have to be careful with verbs which don't change. *You shut the door* could mean two things: 'I am telling you to shut the door now' or 'It was you who shut the door a little while ago'. The context usually makes it clear which meaning is intended.

The most irregular verbs

The most irregular verbs are those where each verb form has a different vowel:
  swim – swam – swum   begin – began – begun
Go is especially strange, because it uses a completely different type of word for its past tense: *go – went – gone*. But *be* is the most irregular verb of all, because it has two different forms as part of its past tense, and two other forms in the present tense – *am* and *are*:

BASE FORM	–S FORM	–ING PARTICIPLE	–ED PAST TENSE	–ED PARTICIPLE
be	is	being	was / were	been

Of course, young children can't be bothered with any of this. They assume that all verbs are regular, and they happily add an *-ed* everywhere, saying *goed*, *wented*, *taked*, *seed*, and so on. But after about 4 they get most of these verbs right.

Activities

A Correct the errors

Here are some sentences taken from a recording made of some 4-year-old children. The irregular verbs are wrong. Replace them with the correct forms in Standard English.

1 They goned home.
2 Did the postman sended it?
3 I shutted the door tight.
4 She has waked up now.
5 You gived him two sweeties.
6 Have you tooken it?
7 The little pig knowed it was a wolf.
8 Daddy have breaked it all up.
9 He's felled off the ladder.
10 Splash has catched a mouse.

B Use the correct form

In this extract, the irregular verbs appear in square brackets in their base forms. Replace them with the appropriate form of the irregular verb, like this: *make → woke*.

Last Wednesday I [wake] up early, as I had to catch the first train to London. I [have] a quick breakfast, [get] out my bike, and [leave] the house with plenty of time - so I [think]. At the end of the road, the chain [come] off. I [get] off, [say] some kind words to the bike, and [put] it back on. Then of course it [do] it again, and [keep] doing it all the way to the station. It [take] me 20 minutes to do the 5-minute journey. Fortunately, as I [say], I'd [leave] lots of time, so the train hadn't [go]. I [put] my bike in the lock-up stands, [buy] my ticket, and [go] to find the right platform. On the way I [meet] Arthur. 'You've [get] black marks on your trousers', he [say]. I looked down. Sure enough, on the right leg I [see] a horrible oily smear. The chain must have [catch] against them, though I hadn't [feel] anything at the time. I [think] I'd have enough time to give them a clean, and [go] into the gents - and that was where things really [begin] to go wrong. The floor had been recently washed. I slipped, [fall], and [find] myself on the floor with a twisted ankle.

C Match the patterns

Each of these irregular verbs forms its past tense and past participle forms in a different way, as shown. In the list below, find three more verbs which belong to each pattern.

blow – blew – blown   drive – drove – driven
shut – shut – shut   swing – swung – swung
feel – felt – felt   speak – spoke – spoken
bend – bent – bent   catch – caught – caught

grow	spin	keep	steal	sleep	split	know	cling
choose	send	ride	bring	sting	think	hurt	hit
teach	write	rise	throw	freeze	spend	sweep	lend

Usage problems

There are often usage problems with irregular verbs. Speakers don't seem to like irregular forms very much. They are an extra effort to learn, and over the centuries many verbs which were once irregular have become regular. These changes are still going on. Regional dialects often have different forms from Standard English. And even within Standard English there may be uncertainty.

- There are a few verbs which have a regular past tense, but offer alternative -ed participles. Which do you say?

  He's mowed the grass.   He's mown the grass.
  The river was swelled by the flood.   The river was swollen by the flood.

You will find both forms widely used.

- There is a group of verbs where the -d sound of the ending changes to -t. Which do you say?

  I burned the toast.   I burnt the toast.
  I kneeled on the floor.   I knelt on the floor.
  I spilled the milk.   I spilt the milk.

American English prefers the forms ending in -d; British English prefers those ending in -t. Also, we tend to use the -d forms when we are emphasizing the duration of an action, and the -t forms when an action happens quickly .

  The fire burned for hours and hours.   Ow! That burnt me.

But in both dialects there is a lot of variation.

- Beware *hang*. If you're hanging pictures, the verb is irregular, and its past forms are *hung*. If you're hanging people, the verb is regular, and its past forms are *hanged*.

  I hung the picture on the wall.   *I hanged the picture on the wall.
  The mob hanged the prisoner.   *The mob hung the prisoner.

- New verbs in the language are almost always coined on the regular pattern. If a machine was invented which carried out the action of *scromming*, we would say *It scrommed* and *The material has been scrommed* – adding an -ed. But if the new verb is based on an already existing irregular verb, people may not be sure what to do. Which do you say?

  I highlighted the passages in red.   I highlit the passages in red.

Eventually, the language will move in one direction or the other. And that means we, the speakers, will move it. The power of language is always with the people. But, unlike political revolutions, grammatical change is unconscious, and takes a long time.

Activities

A Turn dialect into standard

These sentences show the way irregular verb forms are used in some English dialects. 'Translate' them into Standard English.

1 We were beat six–nil.
2 They etten all the ice-cream.
3 She's rang the bell for hours.
4 We give it back last week.
5 I seen it on television.
6 He's wrote a poem about it.
7 Has she took it back to the shop?
8 The toy boat sunk straight away.
9 I rung him up last week.
10 I was sat on the floor.
11 I done it right.
12 They brung me a new hat.
13 Last night she sing fine.
14 The cloth was all wore out.
15 We catched him soon enough.
16 It growed another six inches.
17 They putten it back on the shelf.
18 It swang all over the place.
19 I've forgot the answer.
20 They were stood at the bus-stop.

B Turn old into modern

These lines from Shakespeare show the verb forms of an older period of English. What would the equivalent form be today?

1 I **shak'd** you, Sir (*The Tempest*)
2 His great love ... hath **holp** him to his home before us (*Macbeth*)
3 ... we had **droven** them home (*Antony and Cleopatra*)
4 ... here **standeth** Thomas Mowbray (*Richard II*)
5 He might have **tooke** his answer long ago (*Twelfth Night*)
6 That Jade hath **eate** bread from my Royall hand (*Richard II*)
7 ... and thereupon these errors are **arose** (*The Comedy of Errors*)
8 You call me misbeliever, cut-throat dog,
   And **spet** upon my Jewish gaberdine (*The Merchant of Venice*)
9 I am sure thy father **drunke** wine (*All's Well that Ends Well*)
10 ... he hath **forsooke** the court (*Richard II*)

C Identify the regional features

Here are some lines spoken by Mr Peggotty in Charles Dickens' *David Copperfield*. (Chapter 21). Find the irregular verbs which mark Peggotty as a speaker of a regional dialect. What other features of his speech show he is not speaking Standard English?

> '*There was a certain person as had know'd our Em'ly, from the time when her father was drownded; as had seen her constant; when a babby, when a young gal, when a woman. Not much of a person to look at, he warn't,' said Mr. Peggotty, 'something o' my own build – rough – a good deal o' the sou'wester in him – wery salt – but, on the whole, a honest sort of a chap, with his art in the right place.'*

30 *Helping verbs*

The 'helping' or **auxiliary verbs** assist the main verb in a clause to express several important grammatical meanings, such as the time and nature of an action. There are only a dozen auxiliaries, but they fall neatly into two types.

- Three auxiliaries, *be, have,* and *do,* can also function as main verbs. They have a full range of verb forms. For example, they can show the difference between singular and plural in the present tense, and between present and past time:

  She **is** running.   They **are** running.   They **were** running.
  It **has** gone.   They **have** gone.   They **had** gone.
  Does it work?   **Do** they work?   **Did** they work?

- The other nine auxiliaries cannot be used as main verbs. They are called the **modal verbs**, because they reflect our judgment, or 'mood', about whether what we are saying is true:

  can   may   will   shall   must
  could   might   would   should

These verbs do not have a full range of forms. They have no *–s* forms: we cannot say **He cans go* or **She woulds run*. Nor do they have *-ing* forms: we cannot say **shalling* or **musting*.

The meanings of the modal verbs are all to do with possibilities and probabilities – such as whether something is intentional, likely, or necessary. For example:

  The car arrives tomorrow.   (it sounds certain)
  The car **should** arrive tomorrow.   (it's likely, but not certain)
  The car **may** arrive tomorrow.   (it's much less likely)
  The car **will** arrive tomorrow.   (it sounds as if it's definite)

Could, would, should, and *might* also express politeness or tentativeness.

  Could I see your licence?   is more polite than   **Can** I see your licence?
  Might we come in?   is more tentative than   **May** we come in?

Differences between main verbs and auxiliaries

- Auxiliary verbs can be used before the negative word *not* or its short form *n't*:
  can't   cannot   won't   doesn't   is not
  Main verbs cannot. We do not say **walkn't, *jumpn't* or **He saw not the car.*

- The first auxiliary verb can go before the subject in order to ask a question.
  Has he seen the paper?   **Must** I go?   **Are** they happy?
  Again, this is not possible with main verbs. We do not say (except in poetry) **Saw she a car?*

110

Activities

A Find the auxiliaries

Find the auxiliary verbs in this extract from Lewis Carroll's *Alice Through the Looking Glass*. Group them in a table as: (1) forms of *be*, (2) forms of *have*, (3) forms of *do*, and (4) modal verbs. Pay particular attention to auxiliaries which have been shortened, to suit colloquial speech.

> *Humpty Dumpty . . . looked so solemn and grand that Alice could hardly help laughing.*
>   *'If I did fall,' he went on, 'the King has promised me – ah, you may turn pale, if you like! You didn't think I was going to say that, did you? The King has promised me – with his very own mouth – to – to – '*
>   *'To send all his horses and all his men!', Alice interrupted, rather unwisely.*
>   *'Now I declare that's too bad!' Humpty Dumpty cried, breaking into a sudden passion. 'You've been listening at doors – and behind trees – and down chimneys – or you couldn't have known it!*

B Insert an auxiliary

Here are some sentences with the auxiliary verbs missing. Examine the context closely, and choose an appropriate verb to fill the gap.

1 Where — all the flowers gone?
2 — you help me, please?
3 You — give it back. It's John's.
4 I — decide to enter, after all.
5 I — wish you'd stop saying that.
6 Oil — float on water.
7 Please — I leave the table?
8 — you rather stay overnight?
9 I — go out, but I'll probably stay in.
10 They said they — interview me soon.

- Compare your results with a friend's, and discuss the differences in meaning where you chose different auxiliary verbs.

C Replace the auxiliary

In these sequences, there is something odd about the auxiliary verb in the second sentence. Replace it by one which fits the sense. Note that in some cases you may have to change the form of the main verb too.

1 I've got to catch the bus by six in the morning. I might be up at 5 at the latest.
2 Where has Jack gone on holiday? I think he will go to Spain.
3 I don't think Mary is in. She must be in the garden.
4 Good evening, sir. Must I see your licence?
5 He's bigger than you are. I shall give it to him, if I were you.
6 Sorry to arrive without warning. Will we come in?
7 Can you drive here by 9 o'clock? Yes, I am.
8 The lorry was travelling at high speed. It won't stop.
9 I might go to the party. If I do, I did see you there.
10 I'll meet you in town. Must you bring an umbrella?

31 *Multi-word verbs*

A multi-word verb is a main verb which consists of more than one word.

- The most common type consists of a verb with an attached preposition (e.g. *after*) or adverb (e.g. *back*). Sometimes, two words are attached in this way.

  come in   sit down   drink up   get off
  put up with   look forward to   look down on

- A few multi-word verbs have a fixed structure and have to be learned as idioms:

  take pride in   break even   lie low   put paid to

In all cases, multi-word verbs act as the **V** element in a clause:

S	V	O
They	saw	a glass of milk.
They	drank up	a glass of milk.
They	put up with	a glass of milk.
They	took pride in	a glass of milk.

How do we know that these strings of words are acting as a single verb? Chiefly because they have a single meaning, which can't be split between the different words. We do not *drink* and then *up*. We do not *sit* and then *down*. *Sit down* is a single unit of meaning. Some novelists even write it as a single word: *Siddown!*

Another way of showing that a multi-word verb is a single verb is to find another verb which can replace it, with roughly the same meaning:

Why don't you **come in**?   Why don't you **enter**?
Get off the chair!   **Leave** the chair!

Drawing the line

Look out for examples where it may be tricky deciding where to draw the line between the **V** element and the rest of the clause. Compare these sentences:
     The patient / blew / up the tube.
     The patient / blew up / the tube.
In the first example, the patient is sending breath into a tube, presumably as a health check. In the second, the patient must have become extremely angry, and got hold of some dynamite.

The clause structure of these two sentences is different. In the first example, we have **S + V + A** – the adverbial answers the question 'Where did the patient blow?' In the second, we have **S + V + O** – the object answers the question 'What did the patient blow up?'

Activities

A Make multi-word verbs

- Choose a word from the lower line, and attach it to one of the verbs on the upper line, to make a multi-word verb. (You have more than one choice in some instances.) Then write a sentence showing how the multi-word verb is used.

look	take	go	look	blow	run	switch	care	find	cope
over	off	after	with	down	for	at	on	out	astray

B Find single-word equivalents

Replace the multi-word verb in these sentences by a single-word with a similar meaning. Note that you will often make the language sound more formal when you do this.

1 The plane has **touched down**.
2 Do you think we'll **get by**?
3 They **turned up** without warning.
4 The enemy must **give in**.
5 We're going to **set up** a new nursery.

6 I can't **make out** the difference.
7 We **looked up** all our friends.
8 They **found out** the answer.
9 Will you **look at** these marks?
10 Jim was **taken in** by the trick.

C Investigate frequent patterns

Line A lists five verbs which are often used as the main element in a multi-word verb.

- Make five different multi-word verbs using some of the words in Line B.

- Show that they are different in meaning by using each one in a sentence.

- Write INFORMAL against any which are common in colloquial speech, and which are unlikely to be found in formal writing.

A	get	put	take	go	come					
B	away	by	down	for	in	off	on	out	over	round
	through	to	up							

D Analyse idioms

- These multi-word verbs have idiomatic meanings. Use each one in a sentence.

- Write INFORMAL against any which are common in colloquial speech, and which are unlikely to be found in formal writing.

1 make a mess of
2 keep pace with
3 take notice of
4 lose hope of
5 cross swords with

6 make mention of
7 pay attention to
8 keep tabs on
9 give rise to
10 make do with

32 *The time of an action*

One of the most important functions of the verb is to indicate the time at which an action takes place. When the verb changes its ending to express this meaning, we talk about verb **tenses** – a word which comes from Latin *tempus*, which means 'time'. There are of course several other ways apart from tense forms to express time in English.

English has far fewer tenses than languages like Latin or French.

- There is a **present tense**, which has two forms. One uses the base form of the verb and the *–s* ending:

    I / you / we / they go.   He / she / it / goes.

The other uses the auxiliary verb *be* and the *–ing* ending, as in *I am going*.

- There is a **past tense**, formed in regular verbs by adding *–ed* to the base. There are also several irregular past tense forms (p. 106).

    I walked.   I jumped.   I ran.   I went.

Here too there is an alternative form using *be* and *–ing*, as in *I was walking*.

- There is no future tense ending in English. To express **future time**, the language makes use of auxiliary verbs, such as *will*, *shall*, or *may*, as well as *be going to*, *about to*, and a few others.

    I'll tell you.   I may tell you.   I'm going to tell you.
    I'm about to tell you.

Adverbials can also express future time. Compare these sentences:

    I'm leaving!   (= I am in the process of slamming the door)
    I'm leaving tomorrow!   (= I am still sitting in my chair)

Both verbs are in the present tense, but the adverbial in the second sentence refers to future time. Examples of other future adverbials are *soon, tomorrow, next week*, and *in three days' time*.

Some special uses of tense forms

- Newspaper headlines use the present tense to refer to recent past time: *MINISTER DIES* means that the minister has just died – not that he is dying while you read! Similarly, when we say *I hear Smith has resigned*, we actually heard the news some time ago.

- When we ask someone *Did you want to go?*, we mean 'Do you want to go now?' Here the past tense is being used in a tentative way to refer to present time.

Activities

A Find the time words

Find all the words in this extract from *The Lord of the Rings* (Book 5, Chapter 4) which help to express the time of the action. Group them into (1) present tense forms, (2) past tense forms, and (3) other words or phrases which express time.

> At that Gandalf sat up and gripped the arms of his chair; but he said nothing, and with a look stopped the exclamation on Pippin's lips. Denethor looked at their faces and nodded his head ... 'I parted with them in the morning two days ago,' said Faramir. 'It is fifteen leagues thence to the vale of the Morgulduin, if they went straight south; and then they would be still five leagues westward of the accursed Tower. At swiftest they could not come there before today, and maybe they have not come there yet. Indeed I see what you fear. But the darkness is not due to their venture. It began yestereve, and all Ithilien was under shadow last night. ...'

B Turn present to past

Here is the beginning of a story in which someone is using the present tense.

> The other night I'm walking along Smith Street, minding my own business, and I see your old flatmate Louise coming out of a cafe. She looks across at me and gives a sort of grin, but she doesn't say anything, and nips off very smartly. Well, I'm a bit taken aback, to say the least. ...

Turn it into the past tense. Then compare the effect of the two versions. Which is the more dramatic version?

C Discuss tense forms in literature

Here are the opening lines from some poems. Which tense form do they use?

Earth has not anything to show more fair ... (Wordsworth)
I wander thro' each charter'd street ... (Blake)
I met a traveller from an antique land ... (Shelley)
Remember me when I am gone away ... (Rosetti)
The curfew tolls the knell of parting day ... (Gray)
Nothing is so beautiful as Spring ... (Hopkins)
My heart aches, and a drowsy numbness pains ... (Keats)
My love is like a red, red rose ... (Burns)
Not a drum was heard, not a funeral note ... (Wolfe)

- In a group, discuss why so many poems use the present tense. Look in an anthology of poetry, and see how widespread this usage is.

- What happens in novels and short stories? Do they begin more often using the present tense or the past tense? Why?

33 *Completing an action*

Another important function of the verb is to help us see the time of an action from different points of view, or **aspects**. Is the action complete? Is it still going on? How long did it last? We can change the form of the verb to give this kind of information in two ways.

- If we want to stress that an action is continuing over a period of time, we can use the -*ing* form of the main verb, along with a form of the auxiliary verb *be*. This is called the **progressive aspect**. Compare these sentences expressing past time:

  I **bumped** into John yesterday.   I w**a**s **bumping** into John yesterday.

In the first sentence, the simple form of the verb tells you that I met John once. In the second, the progressive form tells you that I met John over a period of time – several times in the day. Now compare these sentences expressing present time:

  A door **bangs**.   A door **is banging**.

The first sentence might be found as a stage instruction: the door is made to bang just once. The second sentence means that the door is banging repeatedly.

- If we want to stress that an action started in the past and is continuing up to the present, we can use the -*ed* form of the main verb along with a form of the auxiliary verb *have*. This is called the **perfective aspect**. Compare:

  I **lived** in Paris for years.   I **have lived** in Paris for years.

In the first sentence, the past tense of the verb tells you that I am no longer living in Paris. That event is over. In the second sentence, the perfective form tells you that I am still living in Paris. That event is still going on.

Some special uses of aspect

- American English tends to use the past tense where British English uses the perfective.
  US   Did you eat?   UK   Have you eaten?
  You told me already.   You've told me already.

- Different kinds of adverbial are used with the past tense and the perfective.
  I saw John yesterday / last week / a year ago.
  I haven't seen John recently / so far / up to now.
  Using the wrong adverbial is a common error in learning English:
      *I've seen him a week ago.   *I didn't see you since Monday.

- You'll hear many progressive forms in conversation, but they are not very common in the written language. See how many examples you can find in the extracts from literature on earlier pages of this book (e.g. pp. 16, 27, 35, 39).

116

Activities

A Identify progressive and perfective

Find examples of the progressive form and the perfective form in these sentences. Note that some sentences contain both together.

1 Mary has passed her exam.
2 I was thinking about you yesterday.
3 Are you going to San Francisco?
4 Someone has broken a window.
5 We were looking for you everywhere.
6 I've been making up my mind.
7 Have you seen my pen?
8 I had hoped you would stay.
9 We should be going.
10 John has been working very hard.

B Match time expressions

Decide whether these expressions are used with the past tense or the perfective aspect. Write a sentence to show the usage. The first one is done for you.

a month ago: I went on holiday a month ago.   PAST TENSE

1 three weeks ago   2 up to now   3 since Tuesday   4 last year
5 so far   6 yesterday   7 the other day   8 hitherto

C Analyse the use of the progressive

This extract is from A.S. Byatt's short story, 'The July Ghost'.

- Find all the main verbs, and put them into two columns – those which are in the progressive form, and those which are not.

- If you think the verb action is short and sudden, put an S after it. If you think it is long and drawn out, put an L after it. If you can't decide, put a question mark. There will be L's in both columns, but which column has no S's?

- There are no progressive forms in the second paragraph. Can you work out why?

He *was* there again, the next day, *leaning* back in the crook of the tree, arms *crossed*. He *had on* the same shirt and jeans. The man *watched* him, *expecting* him to *move* again, but he *sat*, immobile, *smiling* down pleasantly, and then *staring* up at the sky. The man *read* a little, *looked up*, *saw* him still there, and *said*, '*Have* you *lost* anything?'

The child *did not reply*: after a moment he *climbed* down a little, *swung* along the branch hand over hand, *dropped* to the ground, *raised* an arm in salute, and *was* up over the usual route over the wall.

Two days later he *was lying* on his stomach on the edge of the lawn, out of the shade, this time in a white tee shirt with a pattern of blue chips and water-lines on it, his bare feet and legs *stretched* in the sun. He *was chewing* a grass stem, and *studying* the earth, as though *watching* for insects. The man *said* 'Hi, there', and the boy *looked up* . . .

34 *Active and passive*

The action expressed by the clause can be viewed in either of two ways:

> The dog chased the cat.   The cat was chased by the dog.

The two clauses mean the same thing, but the way the action is expressed is different.

- In the first example, the subject, *the dog*, is the active element. The dog is doing the chasing. The clause is in the **active voice**.

- In the second example, the subject, *the cat*, is receiving the action. The cat is being chased. The clause is in the **passive voice**.

A recipe for forming passives from actives

1 Move the subject of the active verb to the end of the clause, so that it becomes the passive **agent**. Add the word *by*.

2 Move the object of the active verb to the front of the clause, so that it becomes the passive subject.

3 Change the active verb to passive, by using a form of the auxiliary verb *be* followed by the *-ed* participle.

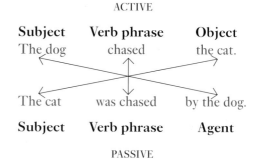

When to use the passive

The main job of the passive is to take the attention away from the subject of the active clause. It gives you the choice of an impersonal 'voice', because you can omit the agent if you want to:

> The cat was chased by the dog. → The cat was chased.

This is especially important in situations where you don't want to say who did something. A 10-year-old might opt to say *The cup's been smashed*, without mentioning any agent at all!

The passive isn't common in speech. In writing, you will find it used most often in science:

> The temperature of the room should be regularly checked.

Here it isn't important to say who should do the checking – as long as someone does it! If you turn this sentence into the active voice, you'll have to decide who the checker is.

Activities

A Turn active into passive

Turn these active sentences into passives, using the technique on the facing page.

1 The police chased the burglars.
2 The downpour soaked the children.
3 A boy with red hair broke that window.
4 A team of lumberjacks will fell the diseased trees.
5 Weeks later, the factory found the missing part.
6 The plumbers quickly fixed the tap.
7 The travel agent is handling the tickets.
8 The students have been collecting lots of cash.
9 Both entrants won special prizes.
10 Not everyone has completed the questionnaire.

B Distinguish types of verb

Not all verbs allow the change from active to passive, or do so in a natural way. In this list, 5 verbs do and 5 don't. See if you can decide which is which.

1 Our friends have a beautiful house.
2 The referee picked up the ball.
3 The contestants lack confidence.
4 That jacket doesn't suit you.
5 The engineer switched on the lights.
6 The concert hall holds nearly 1000 people.
7 Mary resembles her mother.
8 You must return your books to the library.
9 Your coat does not fit you properly.
10 Several people saw the accident.

C Investigate the use of passives

- Here is an extract from a scientific text. Rewrite it in the active voice, and add a sentence explaining where your active subject has come from.

> *Each subject's responses were transcribed from the tape recordings. The directions were coded for the presence or absence of the targeted information. Cases where the subject had been distracted were not included. Agreement betwen the coders was calculated, and was 100%. The results of the experiments are reported below.*

- In a group, discuss the effects conveyed by changing from passive to active.

- Carry out a small survey to see how frequently passives are used in different kinds of textbook. Choose a paragraph from each, and work out the proportion of actives to passives.

35 *Verb phrases*

Most verb phrases are easy to identify because they consist either of just one main verb or of a main verb preceded by one or more auxiliary verbs. Don't be distracted by some special things which can happen.

- The verbs within a verb phrase may be separated by other words. For example, in questions, the auxiliary verb is separated from the main verb by the subject:

  Has she **left** the house?   **Is** the baby **sleeping** now?

And an adverb may come between the verbs:

  I **have** never **seen** it.   I **shall** soon be **working** again.

- Beware of nouns which look as if they're verbs, because they end in *-ing*, as in the first line:

  Swimming is great.   I like **running**.
  Music is great.   I like **music**.

Here, *swimming* is the subject of the first sentence, and *running* is the object of the second. The second line shows that these words are behaving like nouns.

- Also beware of describing words (see p. 90) which look as if they're verbs, because they end in *-ing* or *-ed*.

  Look at that **sleeping** pig.   I've an **unopened** bottle.   It is **unopened**.
  Look at that **fat** pig.   I've a **full** bottle.   It is **full**.

The sentences underneath show that the words are actually describing words.

Awkward cases

A few verbs or verb-like words are not easy to analyse, and you should just note them as special cases.

- There are a few idiomatic phrases which can be used in front of a main verb, such as *had better, would rather, have got to, be going to*, and *be able to*.
  They'**re going to play** football.   She'**s able to take** the job.

- Some verbs with full meaning can appear in a chain before the main verb:
  He **happened to see** me.   I **happened to want to leave** the house.
  I **happened to want to come to see** the show.

- *Dare, need, ought to*, and *used to* are also special, because they can be used both as auxiliary verbs and as main verbs. We can say both *He doesn't* **dare** and *He* **daren't** *go*. But people are sometimes uncertain about how to use them. Which version of *used to* is most commonly used where you live?
  I didn't use to go.   I didn't used to go.   I usedn't to go.   I used not to go.

Activities

A Find the verb phrases

- Work out which words belong to the verb phrase in these sentences, then write the verb phrases out separately.

1 The team must win next week.
2 I've often thought about travelling abroad.
3 Are they leaving tomorrow?
4 Where could John and Mary have left the key?
5 They must surely have been sitting there for hours.
6 I would definitely vote for her in the next election.
7 Will the tall man in an overcoat please sit down.
8 Are we all going by bus?
9 The rabbits are certainly being well looked after.
10 This road doesn't seem to lead anywhere.

- Write another 10 sentences in which the words in the verb phrase are split up. Make them as different from the above sentences as you can.

B Distinguish verbs and describing words

Decide which words ending in *-ing* or *-ed* are verbs (V) and which are describing words (D) in this list.

1 They were asking a lot of money for that painting.
2 The price was determined by a committee of specialists.
3 The new wallpaper is a decided improvement.
4 That's a very interesting point.
5 Everyone has retired for the night.
6 They've bought a new reflecting telescope.
7 You seem to be a very relieved person.
8 The team have been calculating the results all night.
9 Who's been eating my porridge?
10 The police have wanted to speak to him since the accident.

- Make up a new sentence in which the describing word is used as a verb, or vice versa, like this:

      DESCRIBING WORD   I've been to the swimming pool. →
                         I was swimming quickly.   VERB

      VERB   I was running. →
              We've got some running water.   DESCRIBING WORD

- In some examples, the meaning of the word changes from one context to another. Write a sentence pointing out what the difference is.

An example

All the verb phrases are highlighted in the following extract from James Herriot's *Let Sleeping Vets Lie*.

> *The farmhouse kitchen **looked** lost and forsaken with the family abed. I **sat** in a high backed wooden chair by the side of the empty hearth while Mr Alderson **put away** his buckets, **hung up** the towel and **washed** his hands methodically at the sink, then he **pottered** through to the parlour and I **heard** him **bumping** and **clinking about** in the sideboard. When he **reappeared** he **bore** a tray in front of him on which a bottle of whisky and two glasses **rattled** gently. The tray **lent** the simple procedure an air of formality which **was accentuated** by the heavy cut crystal of the glasses and the virgin, unopened state of the bottle.*
>
> *Mr Alderson **set** the tray **down** on the kitchen table which he **dragged** nearer to us before **settling** in the chair at the other side of the fireplace. Nobody **said** anything. I **waited** in the lengthening silence while he **peered** at the cap of the bottle like a man who **had** never **seen** one before, then **unscrewed** it with slow apprehension as though he **feared** it **might blow up** in his face.*
>
> *Finally he **poured out** two measures with the utmost gravity and precision, **ducking** his head frequently **to compare** the levels in the two glasses, and with a last touch of ceremony **proffered** the laden tray.*
>
> *I **took** my drink and **waited** expectantly.*

The extract displays a number of interesting points.

- It is a story which happened some time ago, so the verbs are in the past tense (see p. 114). There is just one instance of the perfective aspect, *had ... seen*, which pushes the action even further back into the past.

- There are several cases of *-ed* and *-ing* forms being used as describing words (see p. 90): look out for *lost, forsaken, backed, cut, unopened, lengthening*, and *laden*.

- There is just one instance of a passive construction (see p. 118): *was accentuated*. It is followed by a lengthy agent phrase. To see the value of the passive here, try rewriting the clause in the active voice, and see how awkward it becomes.

- There are several multi-word verbs (see p. 112). Note the usage *bumping and clinking about*, which is short for *bumping about and clinking about*. There are two multi-word verbs here.

- *Set the tray down* shows how a noun phrase can sometimes occur between the words in a multi-word verb. Herriot could have written *set down the tray*. However, he opts to separate the parts of the verb, as he also does in *hung the towel up*. Authors will make their choices here based on such matters as the rhythm of the sentence and the way its parts are balanced.

It is interesting to note that there are 228 words in this extract, but only 40 of them belong to the verb phrase. As we have seen before (p. 98), the 'weight' of the language lies in the noun phrases.

Activities

A Find the verb phrases

Find the verb phrases in this opening paragraph from George Eliot's *Middlemarch*.
Group them into different types:

1 main verbs with no auxiliary verbs
2 main verbs with one or more auxiliary verbs
3 a chain of two or more main verbs acting as a single verb phrase

*Miss Brooke had that kind of beauty which seems to be thrown into relief by poor dress.
Her hand and wrist were so finely formed that she could wear sleeves not less bare of
style than those in which the Blessed Virgin appeared to Italian painters; and her
profile as well as her stature and bearing seemed to gain the more dignity from her
plain garments, which by the side of provincial fashion gave her the impressiveness of
a fine quotation from the Bible, – or from one of our elder poets, – in a paragraph
of today's newspaper. She was usually spoken of as being remarkably clever, but
with the addition that her sister Celia had more common-sense. Nevertheless, Celia
wore scarcely more trimmings; and it was only to close observers that her dress
differed from her sister's, and had a shade of coquetry in its arrangements; for Miss
Brooke's plain dressing was due to mixed conditions, in most of which her sister
shared. The pride of being ladies had something to do with it: the Brooke
connections, though not exactly aristocratic, were unquestionably 'good'...*

- Which of the above types of verb phrase is used most frequently?

- There are 184 words in this extract. Count the number of words in the verb
  phrases, and see whether the proportion is similar to the one found in the
  Herriot passage on the facing page.

B Compare styles

In a group, discuss the two extracts. Do you find one easier to read? Investigate
some of the reasons for the difference. You might like to consider such factors as
the following:

- **the type of verb**   Which author uses the more vivid and concrete verbs?

- **the length of the paragraphs**   What would happen if you rewrote the Eliot
  passage as a series of shorter paragraphs, or the Herriot passage as one long
  paragraph?

- **the length of the sentences**   Which author uses the longer sentences? What is
  the length of Herriot's shortest sentence? What is the length of Eliot's? (Measure
  sentence length by counting the number of words per sentence.)

- **the difficulty of the words**   Which author uses the more difficult words? What
  makes them difficult? Are they more abstract in one case? or more specialized?

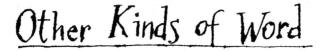

5 Other kinds of word

The noun and the verb, and their associated noun phrases and verb phrases, are at the very heart of grammar. But in describing the ways in which noun phrases and verb phrases work, we have had to talk about several other word classes. This section explains what these other classes are.

A **word class** is a group of words which all behave in the same way. Word classes can also be called **parts of speech** – as long as you remember that these classes are used just as much in writing as they are in speech.

There are seven main word classes in English, and so far we have looked closely at only two of them: nouns and verbs. We now investigate the remaining classes: pronouns, adjectives, adverbs, prepositions, and conjunctions.

Words are grouped into classes when they all behave in the same way. You can carry out some grammar experiments to show this happening.

For example, a word is called a **noun** if it behaves in a noun-like way. If you look back at Part 3, you'll see that there are half a dozen things that a word should be able to do before we can call it a noun. In particular:

- it can act as the head of a noun phrase
- it can be the subject of a clause
- it can be the object of a clause
- it can be preceded by a determiner
- it can have a plural ending
- it can have a genitive ending

The word *cat* makes an excellent noun, therefore, because it does all of these things. But *very* is a hopeless noun, because it can do none of them. Here are the differences.

Can the word:	cat	very
BE HEAD OF A NOUN PHRASE?	YES nice big cat	NO *nice big very
BE SUBJECT OF A CLAUSE?	YES cats exist	NO *very exists
BE OBJECT OF A CLAUSE?	YES I like cats	NO *I like very
TAKE A DETERMINER?	YES the cat	NO *the very
TAKE A PLURAL ENDING?	YES cats	NO *verys
TAKE A GENITIVE ENDING?	YES cat's	NO *very's

You can test whether a word is a noun in this way. And you can devise similar tables for other word classes once you know what the important factors are.

Look out for exceptions – words which don't quite fit into a class. In the sentence *The Swiss are voting today*, *Swiss* doesn't do everything a noun like *cat* does – it won't take a plural ending, for instance. But in this sentence it's more like a noun than anything else.

Converting one word class into another

Many words belong to more than one word class. Look them up in a dictionary, and you'll see them listed under different headings – noun, verb, adjective, and so on. Here are some examples:

- *Carpet* is usually a noun: *We have a new carpet*. But in *I'm going to carpet the floor*, it is being used as a verb.

- *Must* is usually an auxiliary verb: *I must go*. But in *That book is a must*, we use it as a noun.

- *Round* has no less than five different uses:

adjective	the round table	preposition	round the corner
noun	it's your round	adverb	we went round
verb	we rounded the bend		

Activities

A Find the verbs

Here are five criteria to show that a word is a verb (see p. 104).

- it can add an *-s* after *he*, *she*, or *it*, as in *she runs*
- it can add an *-ing* ending (often with a spelling change), as in *running*
- it can have a past tense, as in *ran*
- it can have a past participle, as in *they have run*
- it can be used after a subject in a clause, as in *the children ran*

Use these criteria to decide which of the following words are verbs. Draw up a table like the one for nouns on the facing page, and try out each word, adding asterisks to show ungrammatical usages.

1 know	6 after	11 entertain	16 great
2 clever	7 enter	12 insist	17 proceed
3 admire	8 money	13 trombone	18 happiness
4 provide	9 slacken	14 difficult	19 persuade
5 quickly	10 four	15 intend	20 hopeless

B Distinguish the uses

These words can all belong to more than one word class, as indicated. Write out sentences to show their different uses.

1 final (adjective, noun)	6 comic (adjective, noun)
2 echo (noun, verb)	7 bicycle (noun, verb)
3 dry (adjective, verb)	8 regular (adjective, noun)
4 hedge (noun, verb)	9 empty (adjective, verb, noun)
5 butter (noun, verb)	10 elbow (noun, verb)

C Identify the changes

Identify the changes of word class in these examples. Write a sentence explaining the new meaning.

1 I'm suffering from a fit of the blues.
2 I'll pick something up from the takeaway.
3 They've all downed tools at the factory.
4 He's rubbished the play in his review.
5 She's pooh-poohed the whole idea.
6 Voyager will carry out a fly-by of the planet.
7 Is the new baby a he or a she?
8 Destruction straight shall dog them at the heels (Shakespeare)

37 *Pronouns*

A **pronoun** is a word which stands in for a noun – or a whole noun phrase, or even several noun phrases. Look at the way the pronoun *they* works in these sentences:

Melons are sweet.	They are sweet.
The melons are sweet.	They are sweet.
The melons and the oranges are sweet.	They are sweet.

They refers back to the subject of the preceding sentence, regardless of how many noun phrases are in it. In addition, you can use some pronouns to refer directly to what is going on in the real world: *Look at **that**, **He**'s going to crash!*

There are several kinds of pronoun. Each type has a particular meaning, and is used in a different way.

Personal pronouns

Personal pronouns are the commonest type. They are called 'personal' because their chief job is to identify the people involved in an act of communication.

1 The **first person** refers to the speaker(s) and writer(s) of the message:

    I, me, mine, myself   we, us, our, ours, ourselves

But look out for some special cases, where *we* refers to other people. When doctors ask *How are we today?*, they mean 'How are *you* today'!

2 The **second person** refers to the person(s) being addressed:

    you, your, yours, yourself, yourselves

3 The **third person** refers to 'third parties' – anyone or anything else that is being talked or written about:

    he, him, his, himself   she, her, hers, herself
    it, its, itself   they, them, their, theirs, themselves.

Note the use of *it* when it is emptied of all its meaning, referring in a general way to time, the weather, or life as a whole, as in *It's lovely out* or *How's it going?*

There are also some special personal pronoun uses. *Thou, thee, thy, thyself*, and *thine* are found in older literature, and still have a great deal of religious use. And there are several regional pronoun forms, such as *youse* in Britain and Ireland and *you-all* or *y'all* in the southern USA.

Activities

A Find the pronouns

Find as many personal pronouns as you can in the opening of Lewis Carroll's *Alice in Wonderland*.

- Make separate lists for first, second, and third person pronouns. Do not include instances where a possessive word is used with a noun (see p. 88), as in *her sister*.

- Write opposite each third person pronoun which noun or noun phrase it is standing in for. Make a separate note of any instances where it isn't obvious what the cross-reference is.

- List separately any examples of *it* with an 'empty' meaning.

> *Alice was beginning to get very tired of sitting by her sister on the bank, and of having nothing to do; once or twice she had peeped into the book her sister was reading, but it had no pictures or conversations in it, 'and what is the use of a book,' thought Alice, 'without pictures or conversations?'*
>
> *So she was considering in her own mind (as well as she could, for the hot day made her feel very sleepy and stupid), whether the pleasure of making a daisy-chain would be worth the trouble of getting up and picking the daisies, when suddenly a White Rabbit with pink eyes ran close by her.*
>
> *There was nothing so very remarkable in that: nor did Alice think it so very much out of the way to hear the Rabbit say to itself, 'Oh dear! Oh dear! I shall be too late!' (When she thought it over afterwards, it occurred to her that she ought to have wondered at this, but at the time it all seemed quite natural); but when the Rabbit actually took a watch out of its waistcoat-pocket, and looked at it, and then hurried on, Alice started to her feet, for it flashed across her mind that she had never before seen a rabbit with either a waistcoat-pocket or a watch to take out of it, and burning with curiosity, she ran across the field after it, and was just in time to see it pop down a large rabbit-hole under the hedge.*
>
> *In another moment down went Alice after it, never once considering how in the world she was to get out again.*
>
> *The rabbit-hole went straight on like a tunnel for some way, and then dipped suddenly down, so suddenly that Alice had not a moment to think about stopping herself before she found herself falling down what seemed to be a very deep well. ... ...*

B Compare the use of pronouns

- Which are the commonest pronouns in story-telling? Can you see any differences in the use of pronouns (a) when the author is telling the story and (b) when characters talk?

- Find a play script, and examine its use of personal pronouns. Which are commonest? Why?

Other types of pronoun

- **Demonstrative pronouns** express a contrast between 'near' and 'distant' from the speaker. They are *this*, *that*, *these*, and *those*. We say:

  Look at **this**. (the object is near to us)
  Look at **that**. (the object is further away from us)

- **Possessive pronouns** express ownership: *mine, yours, his, hers, its, ours, theirs.*

  It's **mine**. The box is **yours**.

Note that when possessive words are used as determiners in the noun phrase (see p. 88), they mostly change their form: *my, your, his, her, its, our, their.*

DETERMINER	PRONOUN		DETERMINER	PRONOUN
Its **her** egg.	The egg is **hers**.		It's **my** egg.	The egg is **mine**.

- **Reflexive pronouns** always end in *-self* or *-selves*. Their job is to 'reflect' the meaning of a noun or pronoun elsewhere in the clause:

  I cut **myself**.
  The **boy** washed **himself**.
  They washed **themselves**.

- **Interrogative pronouns** ask questions about nouns. They include *who, whom, whose, which*, and *what*.

  What broke? **The cup** broke.
  Whose is that? It's **the teacher's**.
  Who arrived? **The man** arrived.
  With whom did they go? They went **with their parents**.

This last usage is very formal, and is heard in speech only when people are on their very best behaviour. In colloquial speech you will usually hear *Who did they go with?* But beware: this type of construction is sometimes criticized if it is used in writing.

- **Indefinite pronouns** express a less specific meaning. They include such quantity words as *each, much, many, few, some, any, none*, and *one*. They are often used at the beginning of a noun phrase (see p. 92), and can also be followed by *of*.

  Each brought a present.   **Each of** the girls got up.
  Give me **one**.   Give me **one of** the toys.
  Few spoke.   **Few of** the visitors spoke.

Compound words like *someone* and *anybody* are also indefinite pronouns.

  Everyone arrived.   **Someone** must have seen **something**.

Activities

A Distinguish types of pronoun

Look at the pronouns in these sentences, and decide whether they are
(1) demonstrative, (2) possessive, (3) reflexive, (4) interrogative, or (5) indefinite.
In each instance, check that the meaning fits the definition on the facing page.

 1 The cyclists found themselves going down a one-way street.
 2 The secretary intends to resign. What will the committee think of that?
 3 Someone should complain to the council about the road.
 4 What will get to the top of the charts this week?
 5 Whose is this glove? It's yours.
 6 The question will have to be addressed to Mary herself.
 7 There's a figure standing in the doorway. I can't make out who.
 8 This is the best way to proceed.
 9 The captain couldn't see much in the thick fog.
10 The towels were marked his and hers.

B Fill the gaps

In this passage, the pronouns have all been left out. Insert an appropriate pronoun
in each gap. (Note that some are personal pronouns: see p. 128.)

> *Anne looked at Bob's head in horror.*
> *'— think —'s about time — went to the hairdresser', she said coolly. Bob looked*
> *at — in the mirror. As far as — could see, his hair was fine.*
> *'—'s the problem?', — asked.*
> *'The problem', replied Anne emphatically, 'is —. Next Tuesday — have an*
> *interview for a job, and — think — need to smarten — up a bit.'*
> *'But,' Bob smiled, 'the problem is — as well as —, because — haven't got any*
> *money. —'ll have to lend me —.'*
> *'And — makes — think —'ll do —? — is the third time —'ve lent you money*
> *in a week.'*

C Write a pronoun dialogue

Write a pronoun dialogue, in which nothing makes sense unless you know what the
speakers are talking about. It might start like this:

A: That's mine.
B: Whose?
A: Mine.
B: Yours!?
A: Yes, mine. And so is that.
B: That's yours as well?
A: Yes, both of them. Surely anyone can see that? ...

- **Relative pronouns** are used within the noun phrase. Their job is to link a particular kind of clause (a **relative clause**) to the head noun of the phrase. They include *who, whom, whose, which,* and *that.*

> That's the child **who** was crying.   (= That's **the child** – **the child** was crying.)
> That's the car **which** was stolen.   (= That's **the car** – **the car** was stolen.)
> That's the child **who(m)** I saw.   (= That's **the child** – I saw **the child**.)

The relative pronouns avoid you having to repeat the noun phrase, and enable you to combine (or 'relate') the two clauses neatly in a single sentence.

Two usage problems

1 In the above examples, you can see from the 'translations' that the relative pronoun can act either as the subject or as the object of its clause:

S	V		O	S	V	
the child	was crying		the child	I	saw	(= I saw the child)
who	was crying		who(m)	I	saw	(= I saw who(m))

Why are there brackets around the *m* in the second example?

It is because people disagree about usage here. If you compare the two versions, *whom* makes the sentence sound much more formal than *who*. As with the interrogative pronouns on p. 130, the use of *whom* suggests that you are on your best behaviour. It is therefore often recommended when you are writing. In colloquial speech, however, *whom* can sound pompous, and many people avoid it, preferring to say *who* or to leave out the relative pronoun altogether: *That's the child I saw.*

2 We have already seen (p. 42) that some pronouns have different cases for subject and object: *He saw him.* The objective form is also used after a preposition:

> I spoke to **them**.   not   *I spoke to **they**.
> Give it to **me**.   not   *Give it to **I**.

There is no uncertainty over usage here.

However, in a few cases, people are unsure which form of the pronoun to use. This is because there has long been a debate over the choice of pronoun as a complement: *It is me* or *It is I* (see p. 48). So we find both:

> Between you and **me** ...   and   Between you and **I** ...
> He asked Jane and **me** to leave.   and   He asked Jane and **I** to leave.

According to the preposition rule, it should definitely be *me* after *between*. And according to the object rule, it should definitely be *me* after *asked* (we wouldn't say *He asked I*). But many people feel it is somehow more polite or correct to say *I* in such cases, and you will therefore hear both forms used.

Activities

A Make two sentences into one

Use a relative pronoun to join these pairs of sentences so that they make one sentence, like this:

> I'd like a bike. The bike has ten gears on it. → I'd like a bike which has ten gears on it.

1 I've just spoken to Julie. Julie has just come back from France.
2 The trees look very bare. The trees have lost their leaves.
3 Here's a copy of the story. I've been writing a story.
4 That's the house. I lived in that house a few years ago.
5 The food is on the table. I brought the food.
6 The man is dangerous. The man is dressed in black.
7 That's an important principle. I believe in that principle very much.
8 I can't find the pen. Jane lent me a pen.
9 There's the lady. I sold our fridge to that lady.
10 Have you noticed the player? The player's hat is on back to front.

B Compare formal and informal

● Some of these sentences are very formal; some are very informal. Turn the colloquial sentences into formal ones, and make the formal ones less so. The first one is done for you.

> That's the book I've been searching for. → That is the book for which I have been searching.

1 I think that's the doctor I spoke to.
2 With whom will you be travelling to London?
3 The chap I met has lived a long time in Africa.
4 You seen the poem what I wrote last week?
5 Who will you be singing with?
6 Anybody what helps us will get a reward.
7 The officer whom we approached was not very sympathetic.
8 I was involved in the study of which the results will soon be published.

● Two of the above examples are not acceptable in Standard English. Which?

C Compare with Standard English

These sentences can be heard in some dialects, but they would not be acceptable in Standard English. 'Translate' them into a possible standard version.

1 She spoke to I about it.
2 Me and Arthur had a great time.
3 I and Jane were walking down the street.
4 Us and them have never got on.

38 *Pronouns and gender*

In recent years, a big debate about usage has grown up over certain uses of the personal pronouns which show a contrast between male and female gender: *he* (*his*, etc.) and *she* (*her*, etc.). There is of course no problem when a male pronoun refers exclusively to a male person, or a female pronoun to a female person. But there is a real difficulty when we have a noun which could be of either sex, such as *doctor*, *student* or *applicant*. We do not know whether these are male or female people – so how should we refer to them in sentences like this?

> The applicant should sign — name at the bottom.
> A doctor isn't looking after — self if — works several nights in a row.

The traditional way is to use the male pronoun to stand in for both sexes:

> The applicant should sign his name at the bottom.
> A doctor isn't looking after himself if he works several nights in a row.

But this practice has been criticized by those who wish to see greater equality between the sexes, and usage has begun to change. To replace *his* by *her* does not solve the problem, as that would show bias in the other direction.

> The applicant should sign her name at the bottom.
> A doctor isn't looking after herself if she works several nights in a row.

So we find such forms as the following being used:

> The applicant should sign her/his name at the bottom.
> A doctor isn't looking after him/herself if he/she works several nights in a row.

However, not everyone likes these constructions because they are so awkward. An alternative is to rephrase the sentence by turning the noun into a plural, and using *their*:

> Applicants should sign their name at the bottom.
> Doctors aren't looking after themselves if they work several nights in a row.

That solves one problem. But it causes another – for this solution doesn't work so well if the subject is an indefinite pronoun:

> Everyone should sign their name.

Everyone is singular; *their* is plural. The two forms do not agree, and this makes some people very uncomfortable. On the other hand, because the meaning of *everyone* is plural, growing numbers of people are using it, especially in speech.

Activities

A Avoid gender bias

Here are sentences in which the nouns have been interpreted as one gender only. Find a way of expressing the meaning so that both males and females are included.

1 Each artist should leave his work at the desk along with his application form.
2 A novelist should never forget exactly who he's writing for.
3 We want a teacher who can give his best to the school.
4 I'm impressed by any librarian who knows the names of her customers.
5 We need a new cook, but we can only pay her at the old rate.

B Rewrite an ad

In advertising job vacancies, some writers avoid the gender problem by using the second person pronoun instead of the third. Here is an example from a newspaper:

> Ideally you will have some book-keeping experience, and you should have a strong track record in communication skills.

● Use this technique to remove the gender bias from the following advertisement.

> *We have an exceptional opportunity for someone to manage our accounts database. The successful applicant will be expected to be articulate. He should be able to play his part in a team, and have strong communication skills. His work will include staff supervsion, and he will need to attend monthly conferences at our head office.*

C Rewrite a textbook

Use the technique of plurals, described on the facing page, to remove the male gender bias from the first of these descriptions, and the female bias from the second. The extracts are taken from Betty Byers Brown's *Speech Therapy*.

> *A skilled speaker uses a whole range of emphasis, tone colour, intonation and pronunciation to give character and clarity. He will select his words with care so that they convey his thoughts adequately and then underline the flavour of those thoughts by clear and vivid exposition. The greater his skill, the more possibilities are open to him.* . . . . . .
>
> *The speech therapist has to be able to demonstrate a wide range of vocal and verbal behaviour. She may be called upon to rehabilitate the voice of an opera singer or the language of a man of letters as well as the child with articulatory difficulties. She must have command over any individual consonant and vowel and also be able to regulate her fluency and change her tone immediately and accurately. So her own speech must remain her best equipment and needs the maintenance demanded by any other piece of equipment. It is her livelihood and her advertisement.*

39 *Adjectives*

Words which single out some feature or quality of a noun or pronoun are called **adjectives**. In the noun phrase *a car*, we are given no detailed information about the object. But in the phrase *a red car*, the feature of redness has been singled out. There are hundreds of possible adjectives which could tell us about this noun: *old, shiny, horrible, expensive* ...

If a word is an adjective, you will find that it behaves in four grammatical ways:

- It can appear before a noun:

    a **red** car   a **horrible** fright

- It can be used on its own as a complement:

    The book is **enormous**.   They are **ready**.

- It can be preceded by an intensifying word, such as *very*:

    a **very big** house   a **really horrible** fright

- It can be compared, in one of three ways.

The three kinds of comparison

1 If we compare it to a lower degree, we use *less* or *least*:
    This chair is **less heavy** (than that). That chair is the **least heavy**.

2 If we compare it to the same degree, we use a construction with *as*:
    This chair is **as big as** that.

3 If we compare it to a higher degree, there are two possible methods. With many adjectives, especially if they are just one syllable in length, we add an ending: *-er* or *-est*.
    This chair is **bigger** than that. That chair is the **biggest**.
Other adjectives, especially if they are three syllables in length, use the words *more* or *most*:
    This chair is **more interesting** than that. That chair is the **most interesting**.
Note that it is not possible to switch these alternatives. We cannot say: **This chair is more big than that* or **This chair is interestinger*. However, with some adjectives, especially if they are two syllables in length, both forms **are** possible:
    That road is **narrower**.   That road is **more narrow**.
    That's the **quietest** car.   That's the **most quiet** car I've ever seen.

The forms in *-er* and *more* are called the **comparative** forms. Those in *-est* and *most* are called the **superlative** forms.

136

Activities

A Distinguish the uses

Use the four criteria on the facing page to show which of the following words are adjectives. Draw up a table like the one on p. 126, and try out each word, using asterisks to show ungrammatical usages.

1 big	6 after	11 clock	16 climb
2 canoe	7 violin	12 unpleasant	17 long
3 happy	8 furious	13 under	18 ugly
4 leave	9 delightful	14 satisfactory	19 silent
5 interesting	10 quickly	15 collision	20 egg

B Examine adjective-like words

There are several adjective-like words which are used to give more detailed information about a noun – notably, the 'describing words' and 'quantity words' explained on p. 90 and p. 92. These are like adjectives in some ways, and not like adjectives in others. Show the similarities and the differences by drawing up a table for three of the following words, like the one used in A.

1 falling (as in *falling prices*)   4 parked (as in *parked car*)
2 British (as in *British trade*)   5 stolen (as in *stolen jewellery*)
3 tourist (as in *tourist spot*)   6 medical (as in *medical centre*)

C Turn into Standard English

In these sentences, the comparative and superlative forms are used in nonstandard ways. 'Translate' them into Standard English.

1 *That's the horriblest thing I've ever heard.
2 *Your bike is more nicer than mine.
3 *He's got the most biggest pair of glasses you've ever seen.
4 *The jacket was expensiver in the other shop.
5 *Your writing is worser than mine.
6 *My sister is two years elder than me.
7 *I could play more well than that.
8 *Mary's gooder-looking than Jane.
9 *Your team did worsest in the competition.
10 *Fred's more tall than Mike.

D Make an adjective survey

In a group, carry out a survey of the way comparatives and superlatives are used in advertising. Discuss the way the advertisements use adjectives: if something is said to wash 'whiter' – whiter than what? Are you ever told what is being compared with what?

Unusual uses of the adjective

The main uses of the adjective are described on p. 136. But the adjective can turn up in some unexpected places.

- It can sometimes appear **after** the noun, in a few fixed phrases, and after compound pronouns:

  heir apparent   me included   B sharp   time immemorial
  anything useful   someone important   everywhere possible

Note that you can't put the adjective before the noun in these cases:

  *included me   *useful anything   *sharp B

- Adjectives which refer to well-known groups or situations can be the head of a noun phrase:

  the French   the innocent   into the unknown

Here, the adjectives change their meaning, and become more like nouns. However, they don't behave exactly like nouns (they don't allow a plural, for example).

- An adjective can appear as a complement to an object (see p. 46):

  He made Joan **happy**.   I pushed the door **open**.

- An adjective can even be a clause on its own, by leaving out the subject and verb:

  Tired, I fell into bed. (= I was tired, so I fell into bed)
  Leave tomorrow, if possible. (= Leave tomorrow, if it is possible)
  Remarkable! (= That's remarkable)

These **verbless** clauses are the only ones where you'll find a clause without a verb.

Look at the ending

Many adjectives have no distinctive ending: *big, fat, large, sad, grand*, etc. But there are a few suffixes which can be added to verbs or nouns to signal that a word is an adjective.

wash + -able → washable	fool + -ish → foolish
music + -al → musical	effect + -ive → effective
rag + -ed → ragged	rest + -less → restless
roman + -esque → romanesque	child + -like → childlike
hope + -ful → hopeful	friend + -ly → friendly
space + -ial → spatial	desire + -ous → desirous
hero + -ic → heroic	bother + -some → bothersome
philosophy + -ical → philosophical	praise + -worthy → praiseworthy
interest + -ing → interesting	sand + -y → sandy

Note that some of these endings can also be used to form other word classes. In particular, *-ing* and *-ed* are important suffixes for verbs, and *-ly* for adverbs.

138

Activities

A Make adjectives

Choose ten of the words in the upper list and turn them into adjectives by adding a suffix from the lower list. Note the occasional spelling change.

1 eat	2 road	3 hood	4 study	5 sheep
6 sea	7 shock	8 care	9 coward	10 poet
11 harm	12 curl	13 picture	14 loathe	15 ornament
16 swan	17 psychology	18 shock	19 act	20 professor

-al	-able	-ed	-esque	-ful	-ial	-ic	-ical	-ing
-ish	-ive	-less	-like	-ly	-ous	-some	-worthy	-y

B Change word forms

Sometimes a word undergoes a more noticeable change in its form when it changes to an adjective. Use a dictionary, if necessary, to find the correct adjective forms in these sentences.

1 They sent the troops on a [punish + –ive] expedition.
2 His face took on a [beast + –ial] appearance.
3 I found the committee meeting very [divide + –ive].
4 Their attitudes are rather narrow and [parish + –ial].
5 The children ought to be very [caution + –ous] when they cross the road.
6 We have had an [emperor + –ial] command to visit the palace.
7 With all the decorations, the room looked very [feast + –ive].
8 The story is all about a series of [galaxy + –ic] wars.

C Find different adjective uses

Adjectives can be used in a remarkable number of ways. There are six different uses shown in the following passage. Try to find an example of each one.

1 before the noun (e.g. a **big** hat)
2 after a noun or pronoun (e.g. something **useful**)
3 as head of a phrase (e.g. the **French**)
4 after a verb, as a complement (e.g. it was **yellow**)
5 as complement to an object (e.g. pushed the door **open**)
6 on its own as a clause (e.g. **Tired**, I fell into bed)

The latest message was very clear. 'Send the new photographs, if ready'. Smith stroked his straggly beard and frowned. It made him angry to think that his uncle's clever idea hadn't worked. Anything less suspicious he just couldn't imagine. But now the boss had sent this sinister message, which obviously meant that they thought their helpful employee untrustworthy. Gloomy and anxious, Smith gazed at the house opposite. In years past it had been a church. And now – from the sublime to the ridiculous – it was a pub. Unbelievable.

40 *Adverbs*

The **adverb** is not quite like other word classes, because the label has been used to group together a large number of words which carry out several different jobs in the sentence. There are three chief types:

- Most adverbs are used within a clause, where they act as a clause element (the adverbial, see p. 50). This is what most people think of as an adverb.

  We walked **quickly**.   We're travelling **tomorrow**.

  <u>S</u>   <u>V</u>   <u>A</u>   <u>S</u>   <u>V</u>   <u>A</u>

- But several adverbs are used within phrases, where they can add extra force to an adjective or another adverb:

  It was a **remarkably** quick reply. You spoke **very** anxiously.

Some of these adverbs can make the adjective 'more' than it usually is. Others make it 'less' than it usually is.

MORE	extremely sad	(= more sad than usual)
	really bright	(= brighter than usual)
LESS	nearly dark	(= less dark than it will be)
	hardly visible	(= not as visible as it could be)

- Some adverbs are used to connect clauses and sentences:

  I was unwell, **so** I stayed in bed.
  I didn't want to go. **However**, Mary persuaded me.
  I went to the concert. **Meanwhile**, John looked after the shop.

Look at the endings?

There are very few suffixes which show that a word is an adverb. By far the commonest is *-ly*, which you can add to most adjectives:

    quick → quick**ly**   interesting → interesting**ly**

Other adverb suffixes are:

    side**ways**   earth**wards**   clock**wise**   cowgirl-**fashion**   new-**style**

Some of these are likely only in informal speech. Coinages such as *physics-wise*, in particular, are widely criticized as awkward and imprecise in writing, where there is a preference for such alternative phrasings as *in terms of physics*.

Of course, many adverbs have no suffix at all. Most of these consist of just one element, such as *just, only, soon, here*, and *now*. But there are also several compound adverbs, such as *somehow, therefore, however, moreover*, and *nevertheless*.

Activities

A Find the adverbs

- Find the adverb in each of these sentences. Mark whether it is working as a clause element (CLAUSE), as part of a phrase (PHRASE), or as a clause or sentence connector (CONNECTOR).

- Write another sentence using each adverb in the same way, but make the content of the sentence as different as possible.

    1 I shall be speaking to the estate agent soon.
    2 My parents went to the party; moreover, they enjoyed themselves.
    3 Beth proved to be a very capable player.
    4 I think they were rather upset.
    5 The flag was flying prominently above the castle.
    6 Uriah raised his eyes humbly.
    7 I think; therefore I am.
    8 Anyway, we got to the ground in time for the match.
    9 Put the furniture there.
    10 I appreciate your reluctance. Nevertheless, you'll have to play.

B Turn words into adverbs

Turn these words into adverbs using one of the following suffixes. Note that some words require a change of spelling.

     –ly   –wards   –ways   –wise

1 proper	6 out	11 other	16 street
2 sky	7 happy	12 left	17 south
3 length	8 like	13 special	18 end
4 pleasant	9 back	14 edge	19 ready
5 clock	10 front	15 after	20 crab

C Describe how things are said

Adverbs are important ways of adding detail to verbs of saying, especially in dialogue:

    'Of course,' she said quickly.   Jack growled impatiently at the delay.

Find an appropriate adverb to go with the following verbs, and use the combination in a sentence.

1 chortle	4 snarl	7 repeat	10 snap
2 murmur	5 whimper	8 scream	11 cry
3 inquire	6 shout	9 whisper	12 mutter

Adverb meanings

Adverbs can express a wide range of meanings. The most widely recognized types are adverbs of space, time, and process, but there are several other types too.

- **Space**   Many adverbs can answer the question 'Where?', expressing the position, direction, or distance of an event. 'Where did it take place?' The answers could be:

    here   there   upstairs   abroad   outside   inland   everywhere

- **Time**   Many adverbs can answer the question 'When?', expressing the time, duration, or frequency of an action. 'When did it take place?' The answers could be:

    often   soon   then   recently   just   still   regularly   today

- **Process**   Many adverbs can answer the question 'How?', expressing the manner, means, or instrument whereby an action is performed. 'How did it take place?' The answers could be:

    slowly   carefully   loudly   microscopically (= with a microscope)

- Other adverbial meanings include:

EMPHASIS	I **certainly** agree. I **definitely** won't go. **Indeed** she is.
DEGREE	I **badly** want a drink. You've worked **sufficiently**.
COURTESY	**Kindly** leave. **Please** sit down.
ATTITUDE	**Reluctantly**, we walked home. **Frankly**, it's awful.

Larger adverbial constructions

All these meanings also apply to any other types of construction which can act as an adverbial in a clause.

- **Adverbial phrases** are especially numerous:

SPACE	She walked **to school**.	I stayed **in the garden**.
TIME	I went **for a week**.	She's leaving **in a few days**.
PROCESS	I ate **with my fork**.	We travelled **by bus**.

- Clauses may also be used in an adverbial way, as well as words and phrases. Compare the adverbials in these sentences. In each case you can ask the question 'When did Sue leave?':

WORD	Sue left **immediately**.
PHRASE	Sue left **in the morning**.
CLAUSE	Sue left **when the clock struck ten**.

In the third sentence, the question is being answered by a complete clause, with a **SVO** structure and introduced by the word *when*. It is therefore called an **adverbial clause**. Adverbial clauses are a type of **subordinate clause** (see p. 152).

Activities

A Distinguish adverb meanings

Choose ten of these adverbs, and decide whether they are adverbs of (1) place, (2) time, or (3) process. Then use them in a sentence.

1 downhill	6 seldom	11 nowhere	16 overhead
2 tomorrow	7 underfoot	12 sometime	17 carelessly
3 loudly	8 briefly	13 normally	18 upstream
4 thoroughly	9 courteously	14 sideways	19 awkwardly
5 northwards	10 yesterday	15 eventually	20 previously

B Create some jokes

Look at this joke pattern:

'Have you seen my ring?', she asked engagingly.
'Try that direction', I suggested pointedly.
'I think I'd prefer a poodle', said her father doggedly.

Create punning sentences using the following adverbs:

1 openly	6 ironically	11 dispiritedly
2 witheringly	7 clownishly	12 throatily
3 warmly	8 animatedly	13 shrewdly
4 sheepishly	9 feverishly	14 wholeheartedly
5 calculatingly	10 resignedly	15 alarmingly

C Write a story

The following lists contain a selection of adverbs, adverbial phrases, and adverbial clauses taken from various ghost stories. Write your own opening of a ghost story using some of these examples, or constructions of a similar kind. Aim to write about 150–200 words.

ADVERBS	ADVERBIAL PHRASES	ADVERBIAL CLAUSES
faintly	in the gathering gloom	when the clock had finished striking
fiercely	along the dark corridor	as he turned his head
bitterly	out of the shadows	if she could only reach the door
slowly	in the distance	because he was afraid
sadly	through the open door	although he was tired
reluctantly	after several minutes	so that he could reach the ceiling
suddenly	despite the coldness	wherever she looked
immediately	with great unease	even though there was a candle
perpetually	every hour	as soon as it had vanished
violently	in the doorway	until the sun rises

41 *Prepositions*

A preposition shows how two parts of a clause are related in meaning.

> I can see a tree **in** the garden.　　I have an appointment **on** Tuesday.

In the first example, *a tree* is related to *the garden* by the preposition *in*. It is a relationship of space. In the second example, *an appointment* is related to *Tuesday* by the preposition *on*. It is a relationship of time.

The label **preposition** suggests that here we have a type of word whose 'position' is before ('pre') something. This is so.

- Prepositions usually go before noun phrases or pronouns:

> I went **into the city**.　　The train was **on time**.　　I gave the book **to her**.

- Occasionally, you will find prepositions going before adjectives, adverbs, and certain kinds of clause:

> **at** last　　**by** far　　**in** brief　　**until** now　　**in** there
> I'll take you **to** wherever your friends are staying.

The combination of a preposition and a following structure is called a **prepositional phrase**. You will chiefly find prepositional phrases in two locations:

- In noun phrases, where they come after the noun: *I saw a car **with a red roof**.*

- In clauses, where they are adverbial elements: ***In the morning**, we went home.*

Types of preposition

There are over a hundred prepositions in English, and they can be grouped into three types:

- **Single-word** prepositions, such as *at, during, from, on, towards, with*.

- **Two-word** prepositions, such as *ahead of, because of, instead of, near to*.

- **Three-word** prepositions, consisting of two prepositions separated by a noun: *by means of, in front of, in spite of, in addition to*.

Two- and three-word prepositions are really idioms. Their elements allow little or no change. For example, *in spite of* cannot change to **out spite of*, **in a spite of*, or **in spite for*.

You can tell that multi-word prepositions act like single-word prepositions by comparing the way they behave in sentences.

The bus left	**with**	the car.
The bus left	**ahead of**	the car.
The bus left	**in addition to**	the car.

Activities

A Find the prepositions

Find 15 prepositions in this passage. Try to find examples of single-word, two-word, and three-word types, and put them in separate lists.

> *Ben's room was one of the best in the block. In addition to a wash-basin there was a wardrobe with two shelves and, next to that, a large cupboard. In front of the cupboard was a small table with a drawer, and inside the drawer was a booklet of information about the town, along with some notepaper. On top of the wardrobe there were some extra pillows and, underneath those, some extra blankets. At the other end of the room was a small fridge. He looked hopefully inside the fridge, but instead of the expected cans of juice he found only a piece of mouldy cheese, together with some stale bread. He drew the curtains and looked out of the window. Across the street was a cafe, with tables outside the door. A group of men were sitting around one of the tables, arguing intently about something.*

B Identify prepositional phrases

- Write out the prepositional phrases in these sentences.

- See if you can say whether they are attached to a noun in a noun phrase (NP) or whether they are a separate adverbial element in a clause (A).

1 On the Tuesday it rained all day.
2 She wore a hat with a red feather.
3 Would you like a piece of cake?
4 He could see behind the fridge.
5 Everyone is needed, except Dave.
6 There, on the horizon, was a boat.
7 I'll go there at once.
8 Along the road came a tractor.
9 Is this the bus for London?
10 I opened the door with a key.

C Investigate these words

Despite their unusual appearance (most are from Latin), these prepositions are used quite commonly in speech. Find out what they mean, then show their use in a sentence.

1 versus   2 pro   3 circa   4 via
5 bar   6 anti   7 per   8 re (pronounced 'ree')

D Use multi-word prepositions

Use ten of these multi-word prepositions in sentences.

1 in place of	6 on behalf of	11 regardless of
2 instead of	7 in exchange for	12 apart from
3 in lieu of	8 prior to	13 in addition to
4 in common with	9 in relation to	14 on the strength of
5 in need of	10 in contact with	15 thanks to

The meanings of prepositions

Prepositions express a wide range of meanings.

- The largest group are the **space** prepositions, referring to locations, surfaces, areas, and volumes. They include:

  to   at   on   off   in   into   out of   above   between   across

- There are also many **time** prepositions, referring to points and periods of time:

  at   on   in   during   throughout   until   before   since   till

Note that some prepositions can be used in both senses:

  SPACE We sat <u>on the floor</u>.   TIME We went <u>on Tuesday</u>.

- Other important prepositional meanings include:

CAUSE	He was fined <u>for the offence</u>. She did it <u>out of kindness</u>.
MEANS	She wrote <u>with a pen</u>. I travel <u>by bus</u>.
POSSESSION	That's a pianist <u>of talent</u>. I have a box <u>with a carved lid</u>.
CONCESSION	They drove <u>despite the weather</u>. I stayed <u>in spite of the heat</u>.

- Prepositions do not only have literal uses. They can be used in a figurative way.

  He's in a hole. (literally: in the ground)
  He's in a hole. (figuratively: in trouble)

Likewise, none of these prepositions are literally 'inside' the nouns which follow them: *in the army, in tears, in trouble, in a spot, in deep water.*

Ending a sentence?

Normally, a preposition is immediately followed by its noun phrase or pronoun. But sometimes prepositions can be postponed to the end of a sentence. Compare:

It's worth listening to her.	and	She's worth listening to.
From which book did you read?	and	Which book did you read from?
He's the one to whom I was talking.	and	He's the one I was talking to.

The end-placed prepositions are very common in speech, but some people think that this usage is not very elegant in writing. 'Never end a sentence with a preposition', they say. It is true that the alternatives do feel different: *the one to whom I was talking* is much more formal than *the one I was talking to*. You will therefore find fewer end-placed prepositions in writing.

But you cannot avoid them completely. Sometimes you have no alternative. You have to say *What did the picture look like?* You cannot say **Like what did the picture look?* And in many cases, ending a sentence with a preposition gives a more natural rhythm. For example, Hamlet, in 'To be or not to be', asks us to agree that fear of death:

  . . . makes us rather bear those ills we have
  Than fly to others that we know not <u>of</u>?

Activities

A Match the prepositions

- This extract from Mervyn Peake's *Gormenghast* (Chapter 17) leaves out these prepositions. Decide where they should go.

> against   at   beyond   from   in (7 times)   like (twice)
> of (7 times)   through   to

> *The morning classes had begun. — the schoolrooms a hundred things were happening — the same time. But — their doors there was drama — another kind: a drama — scholastic silence, for — the deserted halls and corridors that divided the classes it surged — a palpable thing and lapped — the very doors — the classrooms.*
>
> *— an hour's time the usher would rattle the brass bell — the Central Hall and the silence would be shaken — bits as, erupting — their various prisons, a world — boys poured — the halls — locusts.*
>
> *— the classrooms — Gormenghast, as — the Masters' Common-room, the walls were — horse hide. But this was the only thing they had — common, for the moods — the various rooms and their shapes could not be more various.*

- In a group, discuss whether Peake could have used any other prepositions in these gaps. What differences in meaning would arise?

B Correct the errors

These errors have been made by non-native speakers. Correct the prepositions.

1 *Keep a blanket above you to be warm.
2 *I travel among France and Italy.
3 *You'll be under deep water.
4 *We camped there to August.
5 *I've known her since three years.
6 *Gerry lent the book from me.
7 *I was alarmed with his behaviour.
8 *They told me on their adventures.

C Distinguish literal and figurative uses

The first use of these place prepositions is literal; the second is figurative. Use each one appropriately in a sentence. The first one is done for you.

> on the roof   We had to go on the roof to fix the TV aerial.
> on Tuesday   My friend is coming to stay on Tuesday.

1 in the cottage – in difficulties
2 above the door – above suspicion
3 up the mountain – up the scale
4 past the bus-stop – past hope
5 through the door – through the worst
6 on the table – on the committee
7 under the table – under orders
8 out of the tin – out of trouble
9 beyond the hills – beyond belief
10 over the shop – over the shock

42 *Conjunctions*

Sentences can be made bigger by joining clauses or parts of clauses together. To do this, we use words called **conjunctions**. As this name suggests, their job is to 'conjoin' or 'connect'. There are two ways in which structures can be joined together, and so there are two types of conjunction.

Coordination

In coordination, the units that are joined are of the same kind – for example, two nouns, two adjectives, or two main clauses (see p. 26):

> I saw a car and a bus.   The kids were wet and filthy.
> Mary went to York and Hilary went to Leeds.

Conjunctions which work in this way are called **coordinating conjunctions**. The most important coordinating conjunctions are *and*, *or*, and *but*.

- **and**   expresses the general meaning of 'one thing after another'

- **or**   introduces an alternative - 'one thing or the other': *Eat now or later.*

- **but**   introduces a contrast - 'one thing rather than the other': *I got to the station, but the train had already gone.*

Note that there is no limit to the number of instances of coordination you can have in a sentence. You could say: *I saw a car and a bus and a dog and a chair and a . . .* However, people usually try to organize their thoughts more concisely, and such sequences would be criticized in writing.

Subordination

In subordination, the units that are joined are not of the same kind. Conjunctions which show this are called **subordinating conjunctions**. The commonest such conjunctions are single words:

> although   if   since   unless   until   whereas   while

But there are several multi-word subordinating conjunctions:

> in order that   such that   assuming that   so that   in case

You can see how these conjunctions work in the following sentences:

> John will go to the cinema, **if** you go with him.
> John got to the house **before** the removal van arrived.

The conjunctions show that one clause depends on the other. Here, the first clause is the chief one, making the main point. John will go to the cinema. John got to the house. To say the second clause without the first would not make sense.

Activities

A Use a coordinating conjunction

Combine the following sentences into a single sentence using one of the coordinating conjunctions.

1 I'll wash the dishes. You put them in the cupboard.
2 John will have chicken. Mary will have fish.
3 Give me a rise. I'll resign.
4 We rushed to the station. The train had already left.
5 They knocked. Nobody was in.
6 Help me onto the wall. I'll open the window.

B Combine these sentences

Combine these sentences, by using a coordinating conjunction, but make the new sentence as short as possible, by leaving out any repeated parts. The first one is done for you. (Note that, as here, you may have to change something elsewhere in the sentence to make it grammatical.)

Mary is happy. Fred is happy. → Mary and Fred are happy.

1 Tony plays football. Tony plays cricket.
2 They applauded the players. They booed the referee.
3 Joan has won a prize. Mary has won a prize.
4 Are you here working? Are you here on holiday?
5 My mother asked me to buy oranges. My mother asked me to buy apples.
6 Emma is ill. Emma will soon get better.
7 I don't know who she was. I don't know what she wanted.
8 I have never eaten caviare. I have never drunk vodka.
9 My sister lives in New York. My sister's husband lives in New York.
10 The troops attacked suddenly. The troops attacked in large numbers.
11 Jenny was born in Manchester. Jenny died in Manchester.
12 They have no books for sale. They have no comics for sale. They have no papers for sale.

C Use a subordinating conjunction

Insert an appropriate subordinating conjunction into the gap in these sentences. Pay careful attention to the meaning. (In some cases, more than one conjunction is possible.)

1 I asked — I could go to the cinema.
2 — the bus had broken down, we all had to walk.
3 The school will close early, — the children can get home before the snow.
4 — you leave now, you'll miss the train.
5 I hurt myself — I was playing cricket.
6 Carry on along that road — you come to a church.

Longer Sentences and Punctuation

6 Longer sentences and punctuation

This book has chiefly introduced you to the way **simple sentences** work – sentences which consist of just one main clause. But the existence of conjunctions shows that there is a further dimension to the study of grammar. You can make much larger sentences which consist of combinations of clauses: **multiple sentences**.

This is the ultimate goal of grammar learning. The true power of the language emerges only when you can use the basic blocks of grammar to build larger, more complex, and more varied structures of meaning. It is not possible, in a first grammar book, to investigate the architecture of these grander constructions. But this final section provides a few hints about some of the things which take place.

The book ends with a section on punctuation. You might not have expected a grammar book to be referring to punctuation marks, but it is absolutely essential. There have already been several references to punctuation on earlier pages of this book. In the written language, in fact, there is no point in studying grammar if you do not devote some time to studying punctuation.

Why? For the simple reason that punctuation marks are the main means of showing the grammatical organization of what you write. Hide the punctuation and you hide the grammatical structure. And if you hide the grammatical structure, you hide the meaning of what you are trying to say.

43 *Multiple sentences*

Almost all the sentences analysed in this book contain just one clause: they are **simple sentences**. Sentences which use a sequence of clauses are called **multiple sentences**.

The chief method of making a multiple sentence is to use a **conjunction**. The easiest multiple sentences use the coordinating conjunction *and*, which can be used any number of times. Here is a multiple sentence which stops after three **SVO** clauses, but you could continue it for another dozen clauses, if you wanted – or keep it going for even longer. These are called **coordinate clauses**.

I have a book / and / Mike has a pen / and / Joan has a car.

In real conversations, of course, we vary the conjunctions and the clause structures – but *and* is still by far the commonest way of linking clauses in spoken English. It is especially important to vary the conjunctions when you are writing, otherwise your style will be very boring.

Subordinate clauses

In the example above, all the clauses are equal in importance. Indeed, each one could stand as a sentence on its own.

Joan has a car. Mike has a pen. I have a book.

But when you use subordinating conjunctions, such as *because* and *if*, the clauses they join are not of equal importance. Consider this sentence:

I missed the start of the show because the train was late.

This has obviously got two clauses in it:

I missed the start of the show   the train was late

But the two clauses are not equal. The second is the reason for the first. The chief point is that *I missed the start of the show*. The secondary point is to say why: *because the train was late*. *I missed the start of the show* is therefore called the **main clause**: it makes the main point. *Because the train was late* is an example of a **subordinate clause**: it makes a less central point.

Main clauses can stand on their own. You could use *I missed the start of the show* as a separate sentence, if you wanted to. But you couldn't do this with a subordinate clause. It doesn't make sense to say, out of the blue:

Because the train was late.

Subordinate clauses need a main clause to attach themselves to, if they are to make sense.

Activities

A Replace the conjunctions

The wrong conjunction has been used in these sentences. Find an alternative.

1 No goals were scored, because it was an exciting game.
2 So that you see smoke, there's bound to be a fire.
3 I was stung, except I was lying on the grass.
4 I didn't start eating or the guests had arrived.

B Alter the clauses

Here are some multiple sentences with subordinate clauses. Prove that one clause depends on the other. Split the sentence into two, and see which part makes sense by itself. Then take the subordinate clause, and make a new sentence by adding a different main clause to it. The first one is done for you.

> My car is off the road, because it needs a new engine.
> My car is off the road. MAKES SENSE BY ITSELF
> Because it needs a new engine. DOESN'T MAKE SENSE BY ITSELF
> The cruise ship has to stay in port for a month, because it needs a new engine.

1 I'll go by train, if you'll travel with me.
2 John left at 3 o'clock, when the taxi arrived.
3 Because Claire had a spare ticket, I was able to get into the concert.

C Decide on conjunctions

- Insert the omitted conjunctions in *Remember*, by Christina Rossetti.

  and (4 times)   if (twice)   nor   or   than   that (3 times)   when (3 times)

> *Remember me — I am gone away,*
>   *Gone far away into the silent land;*
>   *— you can no more hold me by the hand,*
> *— I half turn to go yet turning stay.*
> *Remember me — no more day by day*
>   *You tell me of our future — you planned:*
>   *Only remember me; you understand*
> *It will be late to counsel then — pray.*
> *Yet — you should forget me for a while*
>   *— afterwards remember, do not grieve:*
>   *For — the darkness — corruption leave*
> *A vestige of the thoughts — once I had,*
> *Better by far you should forget — smile*
>   *— — you should remember — be sad.*

- In a group, discuss whether you found this task easy or difficult and why.

44 *Keeping sentences varied*

We often want to emphasize one word more than others, or draw special attention to one part of our sentence. There are several ways in which we can do this. The simplest way is to say the important bit very loud – or underline it in writing. *I told you I bought a <u>blue</u> jacket, not a green one.* But you can also use grammar to highlight the important part.

- You can change the order of the words, putting the important words at the front. Here are two 'ordinary' sentences, using normal word order:

    The rain came down.   They dived into the sea.

Now here are the same sentences with one element made more emphatic:

    <u>**Down**</u> came the rain.   <u>**Into the sea**</u> they dived.

In telling a story, the action can be made to sound much more exciting if you put elements unexpectedly at the front of a sentence.

- You can use a construction which begins with *it*. Take the sentence *John saw 'Hamlet' in London*, and imagine you want to draw attention to **what** was seen. You can do it like this:

    <u>It was '*Hamlet*'</u> that John saw in London.

Now imagine that you want to draw attention to **where** *Hamlet* was seen. You can say:

    <u>It was in London</u> that John saw 'Hamlet'.

Now imagine you want to draw attention to **who** did the seeing:

    <u>It was John</u> who saw 'Hamlet' in London.

- If you want to draw attention to the **whole** of a clause, you can use a special construction which begins with the word *there*. Start with an 'ordinary' sentence, such as:

    Many animals are in danger these days.

    and you can make it sound stronger in this way:

    <u>**There are**</u> many animals in danger these days.

In sentences like this, the opening words, such as *there are* or *there is*, do not add any extra meaning. They act like a flag, signalling that what is coming next is specially important.

Activities

A Change the order

Change the emphasis in these sentences by putting one of the clause elements at the front. The first one is done for you.

> They decided to visit the hospital three days later. →
> Three days later, they decided to visit the hospital.

1 He called himself Emerick Ventrologue.
2 It has been a disgrace, quite frankly.
3 I find your writing impossible to read.
4 I have English homework on Wednesdays.
5 They serve really nice food at that hotel.
6 I was born in Glasgow and I shall die in Glasgow.
7 The marks at the base of the statue were especially interesting.
8 The cyclists raced along the promenade and into the town.

B Use *it* constructions

Which element is being given attention in these sentences? Rewrite the sentence so that it attracts less attention. The first one is done for you.

It's this book that I said you could borrow.	this book	I said you could borrow this book.

1 It was last night that someone spoke to Mary.
2 It's next week that I'll have trouble getting away.
3 It was in the back garden that the water first started to settle.
4 It was in September that my knee started aching.
5 It may be his brother that you're thinking of.
6 It was because John was unwell that we decided to come home.
7 It was a doctor who eventually arrived at the house.
8 It was late in the evening when the parcel finally arrived.

C Use a *there* construction

Change the emphasis of these sentences by using a *there* construction. Pay careful attention to whether the verb following *there* should be singular or plural. The first one is done for you.

> Two large rabbits lay in the hutch. → There were two large rabbits lying in
> the hutch.

1 A lorry was blocking the street.
2 Three points are important.
3 No one was waiting.
4 Something is in my eye.
5 Many countries suffer from famine.
6 The play has some splendid actors.
7 A terrible wind sprang up.
8 Was a glove left in your flat?

45 *Punctuation*

When you say sentences aloud, you use melody and tone of voice to make them sound natural, and to help say what you mean. Your rhythm and pauses help to show which parts of a sentence belong together, and which parts need to be separated from each other. In writing, all these jobs are carried out by **punctuation marks** and **spacing**. There is always a small space after a punctuation mark.

- Words are separated just by **spaces**. Wedonotwritelikethis.

- Sentences are separated by **full-stops** (.), **question marks** (?), or **exclamation marks** (!). In addition, we leave an extra space after these marks, and begin our next sentence with a capital letter. The first example below breaks all these rules, and is much more difficult to understand.

  > We travelled to the city the trains were very busy.
  > We travelled to the city. The trains were very busy.

- Paragraphs are shown by a new start to a line. Some books separate paragraphs by leaving a whole line blank. Others show a new paragraph by starting the first line in from the margin (**indentation**).

- The **hyphen** (-) shows which parts of a word belong together. This is really important if a word has to be split because you cannot make it fit into a line.

- The **comma** (,) is the commonest punctuation mark, with many jobs. It can separate a series of words, or a series of phrases, or a series of clauses.

SEPARATING WORDS	I saw a sleek, red, expensive car in the drive.
SEPARATING PHRASES	I bought a packet of crisps, a pound of mince, and a bucket.
SEPARATING CLAUSES	I went to Paris, John went to Rome, and Freda went to Oslo.

- The **colon** (:) makes a more definite separation after a clause. It is especially useful when you want to link a series of separate clauses in the second part of a sentence.

  > This is the solution: double our pay.
  > I have three points to make: we should act now; we should take care; and we should keep careful notes of what we do.

- The **semi-colon** (;) usually separates clauses. It is the punctuation equivalent of using the word *and*. Note that the separation is much stronger than would be found if you used a comma.

  > I went to Paris; John went to Rome; and Freda went to Oslo.
  > I went to Paris, John went to Rome, and Freda went to Oslo.

Activities

A Replace the punctuation

These sentences have had all their punctuation and capitalization removed (but the word spaces have been left in). Put the missing features back.

1 i think its time everyone went home
2 jack bought the wood from the doityourself shop
3 weve had some good news the bags been found
4 eleanor i think you should get an earlier train just in case youre late
5 have you heard the news theres been a breakin at the school

B Correct the punctuation

These sentences have been punctuated wrongly. Make appropriate corrections.

1 I've never heard of a pig: loose on a motorway. Before? Have you.
2 I shall buy some apples. Plums and pears! When I go shopping I'll make a trifle.
3 anyway theres not much you can do. About it, why are you so worried.
4 Ted flew to New. York ; and Paris but took the train to Prague?
5 I came I saw. I conquered that's. A quotation.

C Distinguish the meanings

In each of these sentence pairs, the presence of a comma causes a difference in meaning. Work out what the contrast is, then write a follow-up sentence to show the difference.

1 I washed and brushed my hair.
  I washed, and brushed my hair.

2 They walked onto the stage naturally.
  They walked onto the stage, naturally.

3 Mark the butcher and my uncle travelled in one car.
  Mark, the butcher, and my uncle travelled in one car.

4 I've got more, specialized books upstairs.
  I've got more specialized books upstairs.

5 Where did they go then?
  Where did they go, then?

6 You know it belongs to me.
  You know, it belongs to me.

7 They sent Joan, our new gardener.
  They sent Joan our new gardener.

8 I'm inviting John, and Sue and Arthur, and Mary.
  I'm inviting John and Sue, and Arthur and Mary.

Punctuation marks which have a meaning

A few punctuation marks do more than just separate parts of the sentence.

- The **question mark** shows that a sentence is a question or to be spoken in a questioning way:

  Are you leaving tomorrow?   I've won a prize?

- The **exclamation mark** shows that a sentence is an exclamation, or one which has to be spoken in a special tone of voice:

  Gosh!   Stop thief!   As you can imagine, I wasn't too pleased!

- The **apostrophe** shows that one or more letters have been left out:

  she is → she's   is not → isn't   I am not → I'm not

It also acts as a signal of the genitive ending on a noun (see p. 82):

  the cat's food   the cats' food

- Several pairs of punctuation marks show that one construction has been included within another. The **brackets, dashes,** and **inverted commas** show which words belong together:

  The prize (a bottle of beer) was won by Arthur.
  The prize – a bottle of beer – was won by Arthur.
  I saw the words 'a bottle of beer' on the envelope.

Inverted commas (or **quotation marks**) are especially used to show speech:

  'That', I thought, 'is certainly better than nothing'.

Usage variation

- Some writers like to use a comma before *and* in a list; others don't.
  I bought lemonade, crisps, and cheese.
  I bought lemonade, crisps and cheese.
  Similarly, it is not strictly necessary to have a comma after an opening adverbial in a sentence:
  In the morning we got up early. In the morning, we got up early.
  But if the adverbial is very lengthy, it can be a great help, telling your reader when to expect the subject of the clause.
  On the morning of Jane's wedding to Charles, the butcher got up early.

- Single inverted commas ('...') are generally replacing double inverted commas ("...") in modern print and in the electronic media. But both kinds are needed to show a quotation inside a quotation, as here:
  'He said "Hello" very snootily,' Joan continued.
  You will find quite a bit of variation in usage. American books use double inverted commas more than British books do.

Activities

A Add an apostrophe

Add an apostrophe to make these sentences acceptable.

1 There are three is in the word irritation.
2 Were going to be travelling by train.
3 The elephants trainers will join the show next week.
4 It was five oclock when the rehearsal ended.
5 Were you a member of the class of 79?

B Add punctuation marks

Add punctuation marks in pairs to make these sentences acceptable.

1 That's a nice car I said.
2 I saw the words happy birthday on the wall.
3 The other person in the car I think his name was Smith looked very nervous.
4 At that time the soldiers if you can call them soldiers were very poorly trained.
5 We shall see below p. 166 that the leader of the revolution was John Jones 1706–77.

C Explain the use of capitals

In each of these examples from John Mortimer's *Rumpole of the Bailey* there is a special use of capital letters. Write a sentence explaining what it is.

1 I, Horace Rumpole, barrister at law, 68 next birthday, Old Bailey Hack, husband to Mrs Hilda Rumpole (known to me only as She Who Must Be Obeyed) and father to Nicholas Rumpole ...

2 'I think we was speaking about the Stones.'
'What "stones" are these?' The judge's ignorance of the life around him seemed to be causing him some sort of wild panic. ...
'The Rolling Stones, my Lord.'

3 I turned my attention back to Peanuts. 'Are you a dedicated artist? The Rembrandt of the Remand Centre?'

4 Sam ignored this and recalled the Good Old Days as he passed me a rum.

5 I told you Wystan never had much of a practice at the Bar ...
Later I sat in the residents' lounge, a small room which opened off the bar ...

D Carry out a survey

The extent to which punctuation is used varies greatly between different writing situations. Carry out a survey to find out which situation uses punctuation most heavily and which least heavily. A good range of usage will be found in posters, commercial advertisements, poems, official letters, informal letters, signs (over doorways, etc.), newspaper headlines, and greetings cards.

Pearson Education Limited
Edinburgh Gate
Harlow
Essex CM20 2JE, England
and Associated Companies throughout the World

First published 1996
Tenth impression 2005
Set in 11/12$_{1/2}$pt Ehrhardt
Printed in China
EPC/10

ISBN 0582 29435 5

The publisher's policy is to use paper manufactured from
sustainable forests.